Vittorio Tessera

INNOCENTI

Lambretta

RESTORATION GUIDE

EXPANDED EDITION

GIORGIO NADA EDITORE

Giorgio Nada Editore

Editorial Coordination
Antonio Maffeis / Luciano Greggio

Editing
Giorgio Nada Editore

Graphic design
Sergio Nada / Aimone Bolliger

Cover design
Annamaria Romano

Photographs by
Archivio fotografico Lambretta Club Italia, archivio Giorgio Nada Editore, Aragozzini, Gian Colombo, Studio Crabb, Vittorio Tessera, Roberto Zabban.
Graphics for Lambretta colours: Studio A. Prestampa (MI).

Final technical files
Daniele Rey

© 2005 Giorgio Nada Editore, Vimodrone (MI)
© 2012 Giorgio Nada Editore, Vimodrone (MI)
   Expanded edition

All rights reserved. Apart from any fair dealing for the purpose of private study, research, criticism or review, no part of this publication may be reproduced, stored in a retrieval system, or transmitted, by any means, electronic, electrical, chemical, mechanical, optical photocopying, recording or otherwise, without prior written permission. All enquiries should be addressed to:

Giorgio Nada Editore s.r.l.
Via Claudio Treves, 15/17
I – 20090 VIMODRONE - MI
Tel. +39 02 27301126
Fax +39 02 27301454
E-mail: info@giorgionadaeditore.it
www.giorgionadaeditore.it

| Allo stesso indirizzo può essere richiesto il catalogo di tutte le opere pubblicate dalla Casa Editrice. | *The catalogue of Giorgio Nada Editore publications is available on request at the above address.* |

Innocenti Lambretta
RESTORATION GUIDE
ISBN: 978-88-7911-551-3

SUMMARY

INTRODUCTION	4	Lambretta 125-150 LI Series II	36
		Lambretta 125-150 LI Series III	38
Lambretta 125 m (A)	6	Lambretta 175 TV Series III– 200 TV	40
Lambretta 125 B	8	Lambretta 50-100 – 125 3m – 125 4m Junior	44
Lambretta 125 C-LC	10	Lambretta 125 – 150 Special (Golden – Silver)	48
Lambretta 125 D-LD	12	Lambretta 150 SX – 200 SX	50
Lambretta 125 E	16	Lambretta 50 C-CL – 75 S-SL	54
Lambretta 125 F – F II Series	18	Lambretta 50 DE LUXE – Special	56
Lambretta 150 D-LD – 125 LD Derivata	20	Lambretta 125 – 150 – 200 DL	58
Lambretta 125 – 150 LD 1957	24	Lambretta 48	60
Lambretta 175 TV	28	Lambretta colour guide	62
Lambretta 125-150 LI	30	All the Lambretta colours	64
Lambretta 175 TV Series II	34	Technical data	76

INTRODUCTION

This restoration guide provides a straightforward means of precisely identifying your Lambretta model and proceeding with appropriate restoration or maintenance work.

In order to help place a model within its period of construction, I have chosen to subdivide the types of Lambretta into "versions" that cover a significant number of modifications; it should, however, be pointed out that Innocenti never differentiated its models as "versions" but only as "series" (e.g.: LI 2nd series or 125 F 2nd series). Clearly, there is no clear division between one version and another, hence there could well be transitional models that do not yet posses all the characteristics of one version but retain some of another.

After having identified the model you wish to begin restoring you should firstly make a thorough assessment of its condition and any modifications that may have been made over time.

In the case of a Lambretta that has already been repainted or that is significantly compromised by rust, full restoration will undoubtedly be necessary; however, should it be in reasonable condition with the original paintwork, conservative restoration would be more appropriate.

What is the difference between the two procedures? Total restoration involves, along with a complete engine rebuild and renovation of the moving parts, full repainting of the bodywork and replating of the chrome and nickel trim. With a conservative restoration, the work will be similar, but the original paint and chrome will be retained thanks to careful cleaning and polishing.

Clearly, a conservative restoration requires a patient, painstaking approach, but in the end the result will be more satisfying and historically accurate.

I have frequently seen very well preserved examples subjected to full restoration that has forever erased their historic patina and originality. Should you be in any doubt as to the kind work that needs doing, do not hesitate to get in touch with me and together we'll find the right way of breathing new life into your Lambretta.

In the chapter on painting I have provided detailed lists of all the bodywork parts and their correct finishes; the colours have been coded using the system adopted by the Lechler company of Ponte Chiasso. You should use these codes and NOT equivalent numbers from other brands that offer no guarantee as to their correspondence with the correct shade; in the case of metallic paint, you should also remember that Innocenti only used direct gloss types with no clear coat.

With regard to the finishes of the various metal parts (e.g. screws, levers, hooks, fittings and so on), you should pay careful attention to their preparation: 1) Chromed: the item is mirror polished and chrome plated; 2) Rough chroming: the item is chrome plated directly, without having first been polished; 3) Nickel, cadmium and zinc plating and burnishing: the item is treated directly without first being polished, in practice you can see all the imperfections typical of casting and machining.

Over the course of Lambretta production, the galvanic protection of metal parts has involved three different treatments: from 1947 to 1953 nickel plating, from 1954 to 1962 cadmium plating and from 1963 to 1971 zinc plating. The change from one treatment to another was never immediate and therefore in the period of transition you may find Lambrettas with metal parts treated in two different ways.

The finish of the crankcase is very important on all Lambretta A, B, C, LC, D, E, F and LD models through to 1954. Innocenti applied a light coat of aluminium paint to make the rough surface of the castings more attractive. This paint (similar to that of the Fiat 690 aluminium wheels) was sprayed directly onto the crankcase without any undercoat and with no clear coat; the result is a thin, semi-gloss and unfortunately easily damaged finish.

Equally important is the use of the correct fittings: we frequently see good restorations spoilt by modern nuts and bolts or, even worse, stainless steel items.

Unfortunately, Innocenti used many different types of screws, washers and bolts that are hard to find in ordinary hardware stores. When possible, you should always try to recover the originals and subject them an adequate galvanizing treatment; where this is not possible at least try to make a detailed list of the sizes required and order them from specialist stockists.

A little secret for getting to know the sizes of the screws is to read the Innocenti code: in the majority of cases, the last three numbers refer to the diameter and the length (for example, the screw with code 71450545 will have a diameter of 5 mm and a length of 45 mm).

Lastly, the maintenance data required for tuning the engine correctly: the carburettor jets indicated in the technical files are only suitable for engines in a perfect state of health and with the original exhaust. As with all two-stroke engines, poor oil seals or a modified exhaust system have a significant effect on the carburetion data and the jet dimensions will have to be changed.

I hope that this guide will be of help to you in restoring your Lambretta and I'd like to take this opportunity to wish you all the best with your project!

Vittorio Tessera

LAMBRETTA 125 m (A)

Number produced
Oct/Dec 1947 152
Jan/Oct 1948 9,517
Total: 9,669

Frame numbering sequence from: 5001

Identification details

❶ *through to approx. frame number 6,900:*
Mechanical horn with pedal control on the left of the frame, square-shaped front saddle in real leather, rear glovebox with key and ignition off switch, chromed wheel rims, stand with metal blade spring, straight gear pedal, brown light switch.

❷ *through to approx. frame number 11,000:*
Electric horn, triangular-shape front saddle in light beige imitation leather, glovebox closure without key, wheels painted aluminium silver, stand with coil return spring, inclined gear pedal, beige light switches. Last examples of version II (from approx. No. 7.500): brake pedal on left side of the platform.

❸ *through to approx. frame number 14,700:*
Larger front saddle with central spring and brown imitation leather (125 B-type), saddle support in light alloy, stand in cast iron.

Colour schemes version I

Body colour parts
Wheel hubs, front brake shoe backing plate, fork, steering head casting, front suspension arms (2 pieces), headset, frame, floorboards, fuel tank, glovebox and cover, front saddle tilting plate and subframe, fuel tank support strap, headlamp and tail-light, rear license plate holder bracket, rear saddle frame support, passenger running boards, stand, horn grille, rear mudguard (2 pieces).

Black finish
Pressed steel front and rear saddle frames.

Colour schemes version II

Body colour parts:
Wheel hubs, front brake shoe backing plate, fork, steering head casting, front suspension arms (2 pieces), headset, frame, floorboards, fuel tank, glovebox and cover, front saddle tilting plate and subframe, fuel tank support strap, headlamp and tail-light, rear license plate holder bracket (to around frame No. 8,400), rear saddle frame support, passenger running boards, stand, horn grille, rear mudguard (2 pieces).

Fiat 690 aluminium paint:
Front and rear saddle frames with horizontal springs, wheel rims.

Colour schemes version III

Body colour parts
Fork, steering head casting, frame, floorboards, fuel tank, glovebox and cover, headlamp and tail-light, passenger running boards, rear mudguard (2 pieces).

Fiat 690 aluminium paint
Wheel hubs, wheel rims, front brake shoe backing plate, front suspension arms (2 pieces), front saddle/fuel tank transverse bracket, front and rear saddle frames, stand.

Finishes

Crankcase and flywheel cover
Aluminium silver paint.

Carburettor
Body and filter bare aluminium, details and screws in chrome-plated Zama.

Control cable sheaths
Sterling silver grey.

Rubber parts
Green bodywork: green rubber; red bodywork: beige rubber; blue bodywork: grey rubber; beige bodywork: beige rubber.

Saddles
Version I: brown leather with branded "Innocenti" rear. Version II: beige imitation leather with "Continentale produzione selle Aquila" rear script.

Version III: dark brown imitation leather with "Continentale produzone selle Aquila" rear script.

Exhaust
Chromed manifold, matte nickel-plated silencer.

Chromed parts

Frame
Handlebar, front fork bolts, floorboard runners and ferrules, gear change indicator, rear brake pedal, rear frame tubes, glovebox lid bracket and hinges, glovebox "Lambretta" scripts (the inside of the letters A-B-E-A and the line below the script are painted black). Glovebox lock and horn pedal (version I).

Saddle tilt locking lever, large front and rear saddle springs (versions I and II). Front and rear saddle horizontal spring-tie-bar-cap and tie-bar bracket, front saddle L brackets and bolts (version III). 4 clips for the support beetween saddle and frame.

Electrical parts
Headlamp bezel.

Engine
Kick-start pedal, gear change lever, round final drive emblem (with red script), rear brake lever and pivot, oil caps.

Wheels
Large and small cap nuts, front wheel hub brake lever, 2 large washers under the cap nuts of the front wheel hub.

Nickel-plated parts

Front fork
Internal pins.

Frame
Bodywork screws and bolts, 2 underfloor bars, gearbox detailing, pin of the rear frame pipes and screws, fuel tank support strap (III version).

Engine
Fuel tap.

Wheels
Bushes and front wheel hub nuts, wheel rims (version I only). 6 wheels small cap nuts.

Burnished parts

Frame
All bushes.

Engine
Large and small Allen bolts, disc with rear wheel hub support.

Polished parts

Frame
Handlebar levers and carriers (if in aluminium), headlamp bracket, brake pedal rocker.
Glovebox closure (versions II and III).
Horn grille (version III).

Maintenance data

Fuel/oil mixture	5%
Spark plug	Bosch 225 short thread
Engine oil	SAE 15/50, 180 g
Final drive	SAE 15/50, around 100 g.
Carburettor	MA 16, Max. jet 65, Min. 45, Valve 55
Ignition advance	26°, 33 mm on the flywheel circumference.

Lechler system colours

Dark olive green	8022
Dark red	8020
Light blue	8017
Ivory	Not available
Aluminium (engine)	Fiat 690

From left to right. Light switch: dark brown through to around frame No. 7000, light beige from around No. 7000. Fuel filler cap: in green plastic with threaded brass insert and separate oil measure through to around No. 7000; in aluminium silver Zama with separate oil measure through to around No. 11000; in black plastic with integrated measure through to the end of production. Multiple keys supplied with the first version.

LAMBRETTA 125 B

Number produced:

Nov/Dec	1948	1,854
Jan/Dec	1949	31,320
Jan	1950	1,840
Total		**35,014**
Frame numbering sequence from:		00001

Identification details

❶ *through to approx. frame number 20,000:*
Heel-actuated brake pedal, internal clutch control, light switch on lamp fairing (moved to the right-hand lever mount on the last 2,000 version I examples), cylindrical rubber stops between tank and toolbox, kick-start lever with vertical spline.

❷ *through to approx. frame number 40,000:*
Toe-actuated brake pedal, external clutch control, light switch on the right-hand lever mount (the first 5,000 version II examples still had the earth switch on the frame), tank-glovebox rubber stops eliminated, kick-start lever with horizontal spline.

❸ *through to end of production:*
Internal rear suspension leverage increased and fixed with screws, glovebox lid support buffers eliminated.

Colour schemes and finishes

Body colour parts
Fork, steeringhead cover and side plates, frame, runni boards, tank, toolbox and lid, front and rear lamp housing passenger footrests, 2-piece rear mudguard.

Fiat 690 aluminium paint
Steeringhead with the two fork support arms, wheel hub wheel rims, front brake shoe backing plate, tank/saddle cro member. Front and rear saddle frames, stand, bronze suppo between glovebox and engine.

Crankcase and flywheel cover
Aluminium paint.

Carburettor
Body and filter aluminium paint, details and screws chromed Zama.

Control cable sheaths
Silver grey.

Saddle
Dark brown imitation leather with rear script "Continenta produzione selle Aquila", real leather available on request.

Exhaust finish
Chromed manifold, matte nickel-plated silencer.

Handlebar gearshift
Grip with 1-2-3 script and its handlebar support in alumi um paint; 1-2-3 numbers in red; nickel-plated fixing screw adjustment nuts and Teleflex sheath trunnion.

Chromed parts

Frame/body
Handlebar, front brake and clutch lever mounts, front fo nuts, floorboard runners and ferrules, rear brake pedal, re frame tubes, toolbox lid frame and hinge, rear saddle to fram mounting plates (8 pieces), front and rear saddles horizon spring, tie-rod, nut, spring cap and tie rod crosspiece. Fro saddle L-brackets and bolts (version I only). 4 clips for t support beetween saddle and frame. Lambretta script o glovebox (the insides of the letters A, B, E and A and the li

below the script are painted black.

Electrical parts

Headlamp bezel, light switch cover (versions II and III only).

Engine

Kick-start pedal, oil filler caps, rear suspension linkage and rear brake lever (version I only), fuel tap (versions II and III only).

Wheels

Large and small cap nuts, front hub brake lever. 2 large washers under the cap nuts of the front wheel hub.

Nickel-plated parts

Front fork

Internal pivots.

Frame/body

Bodywork screws and bolts, front saddle support, L-brackets and bolts (versions II and III only), 2 underfloor bars, pin of the rear frame pipes and screws, fuel tank support strap.

Engine

Rear shock absorber bump-stop cap, complete Teleflex cable sheath. Rear suspension elements (versions II and III only), oil filler caps, rear brake lever and clutch lever (versions II and III only), fuel tap (version I only). Engine mounting screws and nuts.

Wheels

Front wheel hub bushes and nuts.

Burnished parts

Frame/body

All Allen bolts, front suspension springs.

Engine

Large and small Allen bolts.

Polished parts

Frame/body

Handlebar levers, headlamp support, glovebox closure, horn grille.

Left: ignition off button for the version I (also correct for the 125 A versions II and III). Right: horn button with Argoradio script for the version I.

Maintenance data

Fuel/oil mixture:	5%
Spark plug:	Bosch 225 short thread
Engine oil:	SAE 15/50, 180 g
Final drive:	grease
Carburettor:	MA 16, max jet 65, min 45, valve 55
Ignition advance:	26°, 33 mm on the flywheel circumference

Lechler system colours

Metallic blue	8024
Metallic red	8023
Metallic green	8025
Metallic bronze	8053
Aluminium (engine and frame)	Fiat 690

Bottom, left: light switch (with 3 screws) for the early version II examples with the ignition off switch still on the frame. Right: light switch (with 2 screws) for the versions II and III with integrated ignition off switch (there is also a version with 3 screws with an integrated ignition off switch adopted on the earliest examples).

LAMBRETTA 125 C-LC

Number produced 125 C:
Feb/Dec	1950	34,756
Jan/Nov	1951	52,744
Total		**87,500**

Number produced 125 LC:
Apr/Dec.	1950	16,812
Jan/Nov	1951	25,688
Total		**42,500**

Frame numbering sequence from:
125 C: around 50,000
125 LC: 400,000

This table of tolerances and wear limits is also applicable to the 125 A and 125 B models.

Identification details

Version I 1950:
Irregular quadrangular box receiving the gearshift cable engraved with the script "Teleflex", 125 B-type handlebar levers with 59 x 10 mm section lever mounts (rear glovebox with single clasp, first few examples of the type C only).

Version II 1951:
Shield-shaped box receiving the gearshift cable with no script, smaller handlebar levers with 44 x 10 mm section lever mounts, reinforced rear damper mount.

Colour schemes and finishes 125 C

Body colour parts
Fork, frame, leg-shields, fuel tank, toolbox and cover, 2 toolbox bars, headlamp, front and rear mudguards, steeringhead badge mount.

Aluminium paint
wheel hubs, wheel rims, front brake shoe backing plate, front and rear saddle frames (including all the large and small springs), stand, 2 cross members below the footboard, horn support and circlip, spare wheel mount, license plate mount, tool carrier tube and cover.

Crankcase and flywheel cover
Painted aluminium silver.

Carburettor
Air filter painted aluminium silver, burnished body, nickel-plated screws, natural-finish Zama cover with tickler button.

Control cable sheaths
Silver grey.

Saddles
Mid-brown coarse grain, imitation leather, "Aquila Continentale" rear script. The rear saddle may be either square or triangular. On early examples in particular, ochre yellow saddles may be found.

Exhaust
Version I nickel-plated (welded type), version II opaque black (removable type).

Colour schemes and finishes 125 LC

Body colour parts
Fork, frame, leg-shields, headlamp cowl, side panels, passenger running boards, front mudguard.

Aluminium paint
Wheel hubs, wheel rims, front brake shoe backing plate, front and rear saddle frames (including all the large and small springs), stand, 2 cross members below the footboard, horn support and circlip, spare wheel mount, license plate mount, tool carrier tube and cover.

Grey primer paint
Fuel tank, rear mudguard.

Crankcase
Painted aluminium silver.

Carburettor
Air filter painted aluminium silver, burnished body, nickel-plated screws, natural-finish Zama cover with tickler button.

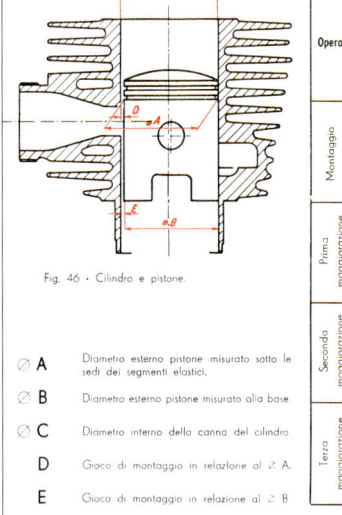

CYLINDER AND PISTON ASSEMBLY TOLERANCES AND WEAR LIMITS

Fig. 46 - Cilindro e pistone.

- Ø A Diametro esterno pistone misurato sotto le sedi dei segmenti elastici.
- Ø B Diametro esterno pistone misurato alla base.
- Ø C Diametro interno della canna del cilindro.
- D   Gioco di montaggio in relazione al Ø A.
- E   Gioco di montaggio in relazione al Ø B.

Intake manifold (sheet aluminium)
Clean semi-gloss (neither polished nor painted).

Control cable sheaths
Silver grey.

Saddle
Mid-brown coarse grain, imitation leather, "Aquila Continentale" rear script. The rear saddle may be either square or triangular. On early examples in particular, ochre yellow saddles may be found.

Exhaust
Version I nickel-plated (welded type), version II opaque black (removable type).

Chromed parts

Frame/body
Handlebars and fittings (screws, caps) steeringhead cable clip, passenger's footrests (optional on C model), brake pedal, upper steering bearing support plate (LC only).

Electrical parts
Front and rear lamp bezels, horn cover, light switch cover.

Engine
Kick-start pedal.

Wheels
Large cap nuts (2 front, 1 rear).

Nickel-plated parts

Front fork
Front wheel carriers, screws and pins, lower steering bearing seat.

Frame/body
All screws and bolts, lubricators.

Electrical parts
Light switch cover screws.

Engine
Levers, studs, screws, oil caps, damper cover, exhaust (non-opening version I only), complete Teleflex sheath.

Wheels
Small cap nuts, open nuts, bushes, wheel hub brake levers.

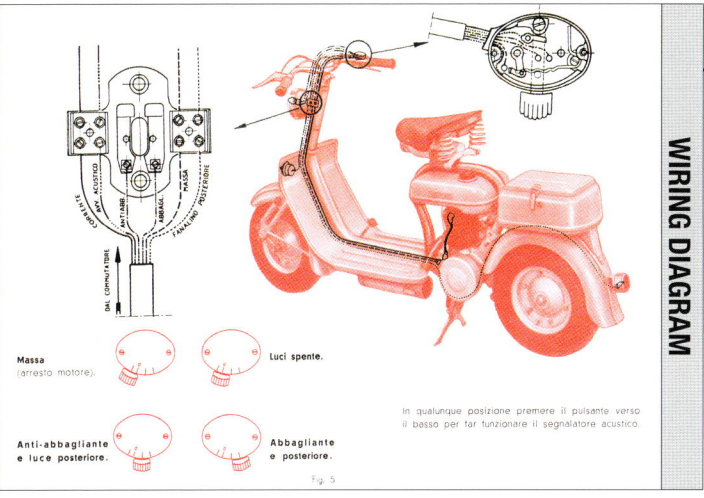

Burnished parts

Frame/body
Large and small Allen bolts.

Engine
Large and small springs.

Polished parts

Frame/body
Handlebar levers. Floorboard runners.

Lechler system colours

Light olive khaki	8027
Chamois	8011
Blue	not available (only on earliest 125 C examples)
Red	not available (only on earliest 125 C examples)
Special blue	not available (only on earliest 125 LC examples)
Aluminium (engine and frame)	Fiat 690

Maintenance data

Fuel/oil mixture:	5%
Spark plug:	Bosch 225 short thread
Engine oil:	SAE 15/50, 180 g
Final drive:	grease
Carburettor:	Dell'Orto MA 16, max jet 65, min 45 Valve 55
	Zenith, max jet 80/84, min jet 40
Ignition advance:	26º, 33-35 mm on the flywheel circumference

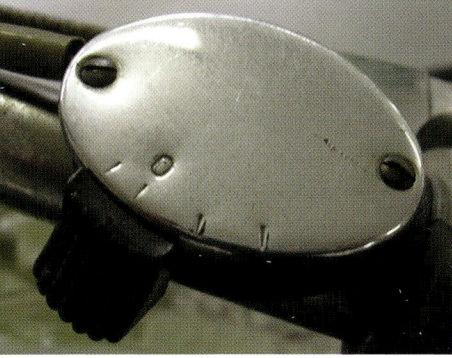

Light switch with black ground and chromed cover used throughout production of the C-LC. Note that the cover is oval and lacks the tab where the cables exit and that the O is to the left. The switch for the D-LD '52 model is identical apart from the O on the right.

LAMBRETTA 125 D-LD

Number produced: 125 D		
Dec	1951	3,865
Jan/Dec	1952	64,676
Jan/Dec	1953	23,024
Jan/Oct	1954	31,076
May/June	1955	350
Total		**122,991**

Number produced: 125 LD		
Dec	1951	137
Jan/Dec	1952	29,471
Jan/Dec	1953	45,796
Jan/Dec	1954	32,927
Jan/Oct	1955	2,003
Total:		**110,334**

Number produced: 125 LD electric start:		
Feb/Dec 1954		8,694

Frame numbering sequence from: 00.001

Identification details

Version I 1951-1952

Handlebar in chromed steel with aluminium end caps, small front brake (125 C type), rod-actuated rear brake with small pedal (modified from mid-1952 with cable operation and larger pedal), saddle frame with 25 C-type conical tool carrier tube (modified from mid-1952 with new saddle frame with cylindrical tool carrier tube and cap closed with a clip), black 2-position light switch with chrome cover, horn with "flower" grille. Smooth fork covers (from mid-1952 with an indent to contain the larger bushes). Engine mounted on plain bearings (Silent Blocs from mid-1952).

Earliest examples of the 125 D: rear toolbox with small 125 C-type clasps.

Earliest examples of the 125 D-LD: a second porthole on the engine cover close to the torsion bar mount that was intended to permit the fitting of a return damper never actually adopted.

LD only: side covers with portholes with chrome rings, "Lambretta" script in aluminium on the leg-shield and the "Innocenti" badge above the headlamp.

Version II 1953

Adjustable handlebar in aluminium with plastic levers, front brake enlarged to 125 mm, passenger grab-handle incorporated in rear saddle, 2-position light switch in ivory-colour plastic, horn with traditional grille (from around February 1953).

D only: toolbox lid lock with cover.

LD only: side panels with plastic air vent grilles (version I panels were fitted to the earliest examples of the '53 LD), plastic "LD" shield badge on the leg-shield.

Detail of the electric start control; the protective tubes covering the cables are typical of the examples produced in late 1954.

Version III 1954
Cable adjusters on the clutch and front brake levers, dark green saddle covers, front position light and 3-position white light switch with chrome cover (from mid-1954), grips with hand-shields.

LD only
New, larger saddles closed at the front introduced around mi-1954, fitted with dark green covers and bi-conical rather than conical springs; in this case the tool carrier tube was replaced with a triangular toolbox mounted on the rear mudguard. Rubber handlebar control cable sheaths introduced towards the end of 1954.

Final batch 1955
Handlebar in chrome-plated steel (still adjustable and with plastic levers), lubricator on the front fork stems.

LD only
Larger 150 D-type carburettor air filter.

Final examples
Provision for a rear damper on the transmission housing.

Colour schemes and finishes 125D

Body colour parts
Fork, fork covers, frame, leg-shield, fuel tank, toolbox and cover, 2 glovebox cross-members, headlamp, front and rear mudguards, steeringhead badge mount.

Aluminium paint
Wheel hubs, wheel rims, front brake shoe backing plate, front and rear saddle frames (including all large and small springs), stand, 2 underfloor cross-members, spare wheel holder, license plate holder and its tool tube strut and cover, torsion bar lever.

Crankcase and flywheel cover
Aluminium paint.

Carburettor
Air filter painted aluminium silver, burnished body, nickel-plated screws and fittings, bare aluminium cover and "tickler".

Control cable sheaths
Grey, nickel-plated Teleflex sheath (cadmium-plated from mid-1954).

Saddles
mid-brown, coarse grain imitation leather, "Aquila Continentale" rear script. The rear saddle may be either triangular or rectangular (1951-52 only). From 1954, dark green, fine grain imitation leather with "Innocenti" rear script.

Silencer
Matte black.

Colour schemes and finishes 125 LD

Body colour parts
Fork, fork covers, frame, leg-shields, headlamp surround, side panels, passenger running boards, front mudguard.

Aluminium paint
Wheel hubs, wheel rims, front brake shoe backing plate, front and rear saddle frames (including the large and small springs; in some cases the large springs are chromed), stand, spare wheel holder, license-plate holder and supports, tool-carrier tube and its cover, torsion bar lever.

Grey primer paint
Fuel tank, rear mudguard.

Crankcase
Aluminium paint.

Intake manifold (in sheet aluminium)
Clean, semi-gloss (neither polished nor painted).

The electric start battery mount. The support swings out to facilitate removal of the tyre.

Light switch from the 1953 to early '54 version; all in light beige plastic with two positions, dipped and main beam.

Carburettor
Air filter painted aluminium silver, burnished body, nickel-plated screws and fittings, bare aluminium cover with "tickler".

Control cable sheaths
Grey.

Saddles
Mid-brown, coarse grain imitation leather with "Aquila Continentale" rear script. The rear saddle may be either triangular or rectangular (1951-52 only). From 1954, dark green, fine grain imitation leather with "Innocenti" rear script.

Silencer
Matte black.

Chromed parts

Frame
Handlebar (if in steel) and its details, brake pedal. Bolts on central handlebar mount (1953-1954). Passenger's footrest support rod and steeringhead cable clip (125 D only). Rear glovebox lock cover (125 D 1953-1954 only). Steeringhead upper bearing support plate, floorboard runners and fittings (125 LD only). Front saddle bi-conical springs and rear saddle spring-tie-bar-cap (LD model only with closed-front saddles).

Electrical parts
Headlamp and tail lamp surrounds, horn grille, light switch cover (from 1954).

Engine
Kick-start pedal.

Wheels
Large cap nuts.

Nickel-plated parts (until mid-'54) - cadmium-plated parts (from mid-'54)

Front fork
Front wheel carriers, screws and pins, steeringhead upper bush.

Frame
All screws and bolts, lubricators, steeringhead lower bearing cap, torsion bar figure-of-eight clip, special washers, bushes, rear brake elements (I version).

Electrical parts
Horn stem and clip (125 D only), light switch cover screws.

Engine
Levers, studs, screws, oil plugs, engine bearing (model with Silent Blocs), engine bearing dust caps (model with plain bearings). Complete Teleflex sheath.

Wheels
Small cap nuts, bushes, wheel hub brake levers.

Attention: towards mid-1954 cadmium plating (similar to white zinc) was introduced in place of nickel plating. This new treatment was adopted once the stock of nickel-plated material was exhausted; it is therefore possible to find 1954 Lambrettas with both nickel- and cadmium-plated parts.

Burnished parts

Engine
Large and small Allen bolts.

Polished parts

Frame
Handlebar levers and grip caps (1951-52 only). Side-panel levers (LD only). Handlebar, central clamp and lever carriers (1953-1954). Floorboard runners.

WIRING DIAGRAM WITH STARTER MOTOR - VERSION II

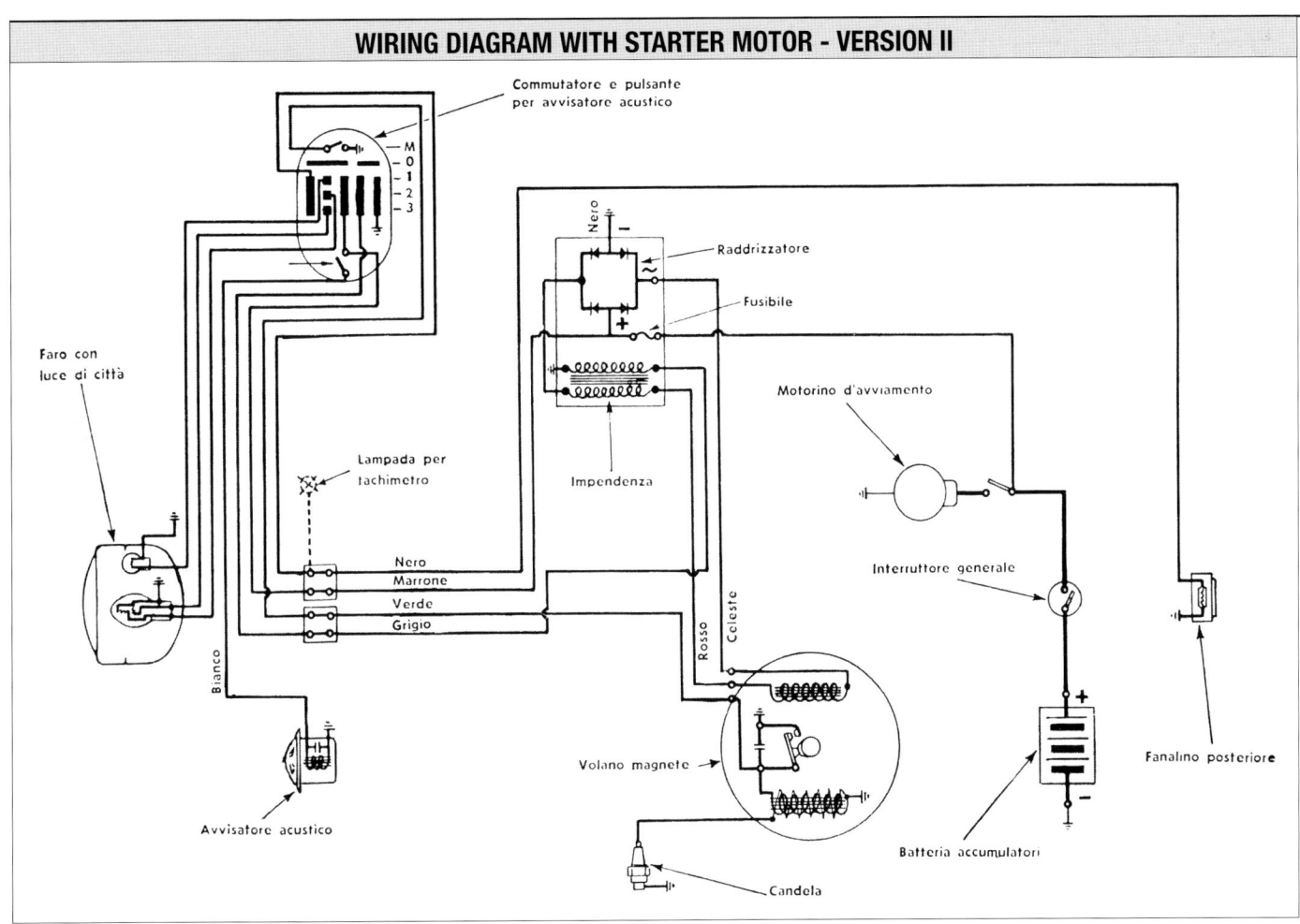

Lechler system colours

Olive green	8021
Light chamois	8055
Sand beige	8029
Aluminium (engine and frame)	Fiat 690

LD model only from 1953 the only colour available was Sand beige 8029.

Maintenance data

Fuel/oil mixture:	5%
Spark plug:	Bosch 225 short thread
Engine oil:	SAE 15/50, 400 g
Final drive:	SAE 140 100 g.
Carburettor:	Dell'Orto MA 18B2 max jet 75, min 40 Valve 50
Carburettor:	Dell'Orto MA 18B3 max jet 70, min 45 Valve 75
Carburettor:	Zenith 18, max jet 102
Marelli ignition advance:	34-36.5 mm on flywheel circumference
Filso ignition advance:	32-34 mm on flywheel circumference

Number produced:	
Apr/Dec 1953	37,572
Jan/Feb 1954	4,780
Total	42,352

Frame numbering sequence from: 00.001

LAMBRETTA 125 E

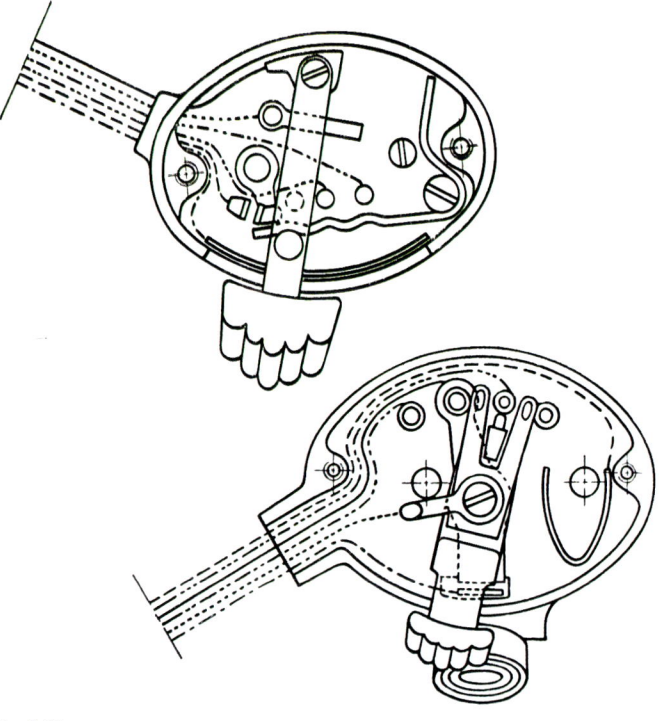

Top right. Diagram of the two light switches mounted on the 125 E. The one at the top is identical to that of the '53 D-LD while the one below has a separate horn button and a chromed cover. Both were two-position switches.

Identification details

Earliest examples
Teleflex cable support on engine fixed with a single stud bolt, engine number written with electric pen on transmission housing, sand-cast transmission casing.

Version I to middle of production run
Ignition advance control with lever on crankcase, glovebox cover with no clips and only a central lock, leg-shield and rear mudguard welded to the frame.

Version II to end of production
Flywheel with automatic advance, glovebox lid with lateral clasps and central lock, leg-shield and rear mudguard fixed to the frame with screws, front mudguard with supplementary support struts, silencer with right-hand exhaust (last examples only).

Colour schemes and finishes 125 E

Body colour parts
Fork, fork covers, frame, leg-shield, fuel tank, glovebox and cover, 2 glovebox cross-members, headlamp, front and rear mudguards, steeringhead badge mount (version with metal mount only).

Aluminium paint
Wheel hubs, wheel rims, front brake shoe backing plate, front and rear saddle frames (including all large and small springs), stand, spare wheel holder, torsion bar lever (on left, below floorboards).

Crankcase
Aluminium paint.

Carburettor
Air filter grille nickel-plated, bare aluminium body and "tickler", nickel-plated screws and fittings.

Control cable sheaths
Grey.

Saddles
Mid-brown, coarse grain imitation leather, "Aquila Continentale" rear script.

Silencer
Body matte black, chromed header pipe and circlip.

Chromed parts

Frame
Handlebar and its details, brake pedal. Rear glovebox lock cover, passenger grab-handle. Passenger footrest support bracket (optional).

Electrical parts
Headlamp and tail lamp surrounds, horn grille.

Engine
Exhaust header pipe and circlip.

Nickel-plated parts

Front fork
Front wheel carriers and nuts.

Frame
All screws and bolts, steeringhead lower bearing cap, special washers, bushes, torsion bar lever (on right below gear change control.

Electrical parts
Light switch cover screws, horn bracket.

Engine
Levers, studs, screws, oil plugs, complete Teleflex sheath.

Wheels
Nuts, bushes, wheel hub brake levers.

Burnished parts

Engine
Allen bolts.

Polished parts

Frame
Headlamp bracket.

Lechler system colours

Olive green	8021
Aluminium (engine and frame)	Fiat 690

Maintenance data

Fuel/oil mixture:	5%
Spark plug:	Bosch 225 short thread
Engine oil:	SAE 15/50, 300 g
Final drive:	SAE 140 100 g.
Carburettor:	Dell'Orto MU 14B1, max jet 68 Jet 268B - Valve 50
Ignition advance	25°, 24.5 mm on flywheel circumference

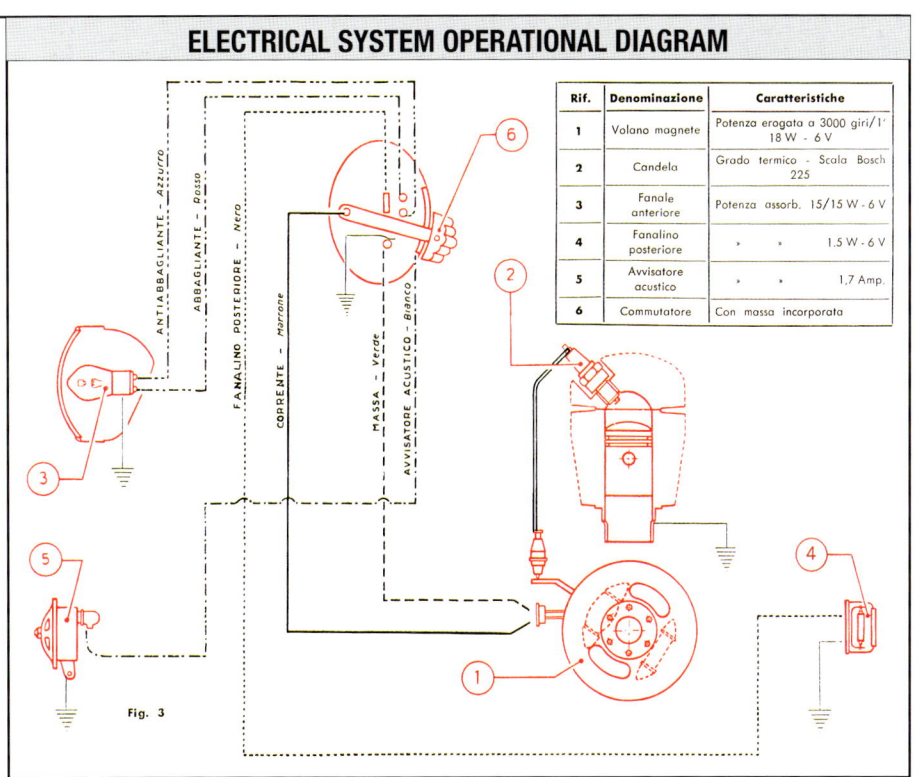

Fig. 3

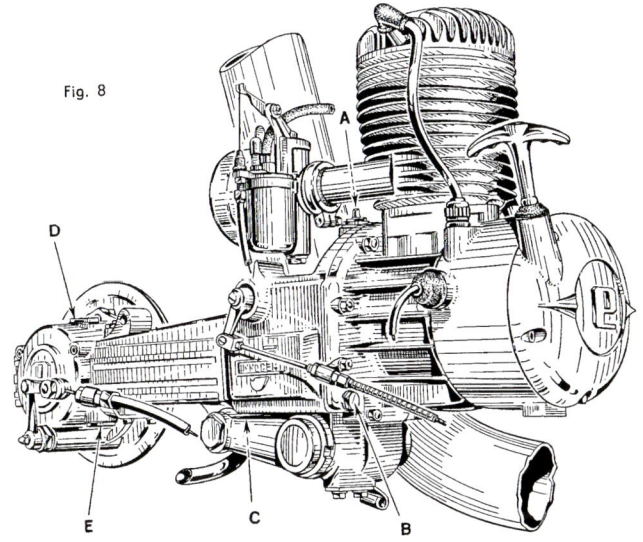

Fig. 8

A. Transmission oil filler cap
B. Transmission oil level cap
C. Transmission oil drain plug
D. Final drive oil filler cap
E. Final drive oil drain plug

LAMBRETTA 125 F - F II SERIES

Number produced 125F
Mar/Dec 1954 26,709
Jan/Apr 1955 5,992
Total 32,701

Frame numbering sequence from: around 43,000

Identification details

Earliest examples
Lambretta 125 E models transformed into the F version by replacing the starter mechanism, the floorboards and the transmission casing. Frame number still carries letter E; later the lower stem was ground down to form the letter F. These examples have the same colour schemes and saddle colour as the 125 E.

Version I Apr-May 1954
Frames and saddles as the 125 E (with clipped horizontal spring), dark green saddle. A transitional model that according to the period of production may have the 125 E colour scheme with the basic Sand Beige paintwork or that of the version II, but again with Sand Beige paintwork.

Version II mid-1954 to end 1954
Saddle frames as for the 150D (front saddle with chromed conical springs).

F version II (official designation)
D-type front fork, raised handlebar, external HT coil and capacitor, headlamp bracket with steering lock fitting.

Colour schemes and finishes 125 F
(with the exclusion of the earliest examples identical to the type-E)

Body colour parts
Fork, fork covers, frame, leg-shield, fuel tank, glovebox and cover, 2 glovebox cross-members, headlamp, front and rear mudguards, steeringhead badge mount (version with metal mount only), wheel hubs, wheel rims, front brake shoe backing plate, front and rear saddle frames, stand, spare wheel holder, torsion bar lever (on left, below floorboards).

Crankcase
Aluminium paint.

Carburettor
Air filter grille cadmium-plated, bare aluminium body and "tickler", cadmium-plated screws and fittings.

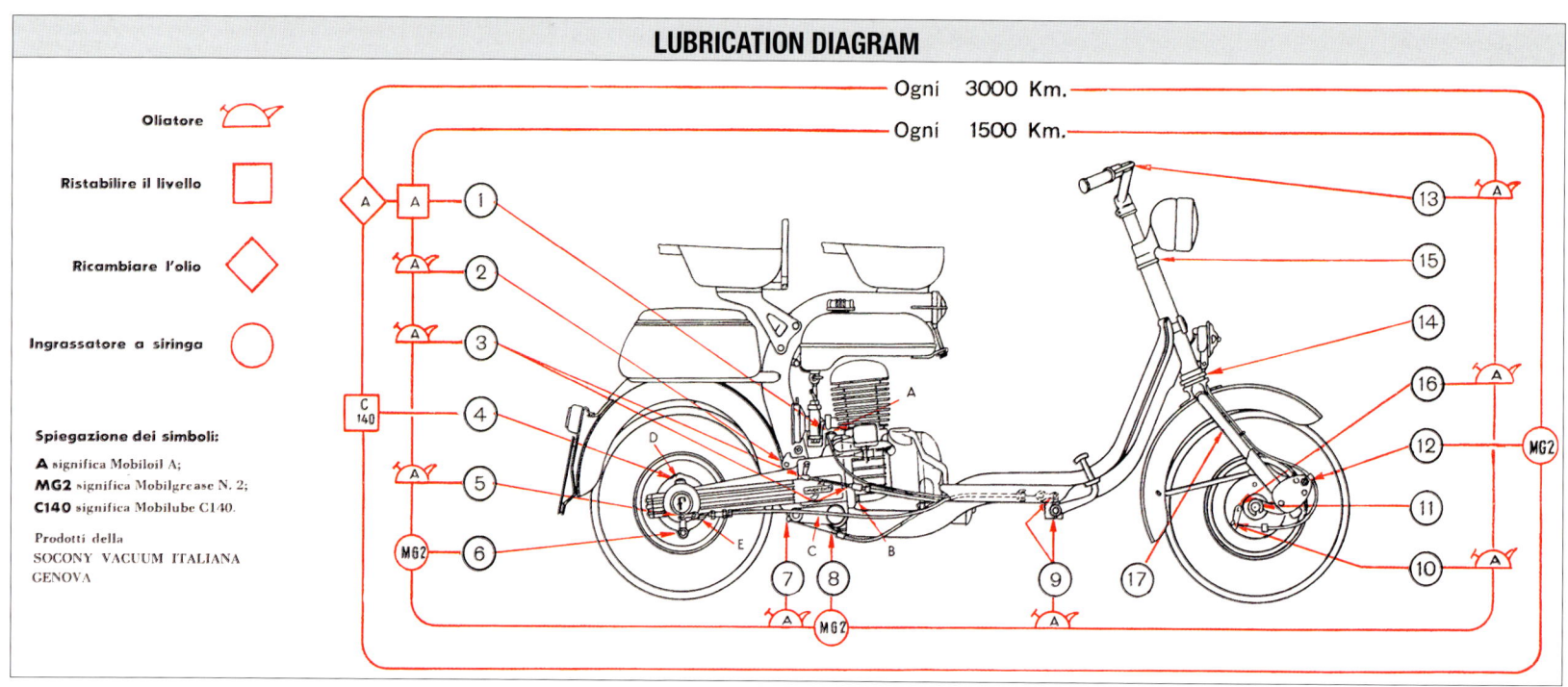

Control cable sheaths
Grey.

Saddles
Dark green, fine grain imitation leather, "Innocenti" rear script.

Silencer
Body matte black, chromed header pipe and circlip.

Chromed parts

Frame
Handlebar and its details, brake pedal, rear glovebox lock cover, front saddle conical spring, rear saddle spring-tie-bar-cap (II version e II series), passenger grab-handle (version with type-E saddle only), passenger footrest support bracket (optional).

Electrical parts
Headlamp and tail lamp surrounds, horn grille.

Engine
Exhaust header pipe and circlip, kick-start lever.

Cadmium-plated parts
(nickel-plated earliest type-E examples only):

Front fork
Front wheel carriers and nuts.

Frame
All screws and bolts, lubricator, steeringhead lower bearing cap, special washers, bushes, torsion bar lever (on right below gear change control.

Electrical parts
Light switch cover screws, horn bracket.

Engine
Levers, studs, screws, oil plugs, complete Teleflex sheath.

Wheels
Nuts, bushes, wheel hub brake levers.

Burnished parts

Engine
Allen bolts.

Polished parts

Frame
Headlamp bracket.

Lechler system colours

Olive green	8021
Sand Beige	8029
Light grey	8012 (a number of version II examples only)
Aluminium (engine and frame)	Fiat 690

Maintenance data

Fuel/oil mixture:	5%
Spark plug:	Bosch 225 short thread
Engine oil:	SAE 15/50, 300 g
Final drive:	SAE 140 100 g.
Carburettor:	Dell'Orto MU 14C1, max jet 72 Jet 270 - Valve 40
Ignition advance:	25°, 24.5 mm on flywheel circumference.

Right: dark red Innocenti emblem with gold script and beige plastic support. Left: detail of the sliding gear transmission. Attention: the screw on the head of the gearlever does not serve to lock the external lever but rather the internal one. If the screw is loosened with the casing mounted the internal lever will drop into the casing that will have to be dismantled completely to recover the lever.

LAMBRETTA 150 D-LD
125 LD DERIVATA

Number produced: 150 D
Oct/Dec	1954	610
Jan/Dec	1955	33,148
Jan/Dec	1956	20,835
Total		**54,593**

Number produced: 150 LD
Nov/Dec	1954	421
Jan/Dec	1955	52,297
Jan/Dec	1956	51,748
Jan	1957	4,878
Total:		**109,344**

**Number produced:
150 LD electric start**
Sep/Nov	1955	59
Jan/Nov	1956	1,961
Total:		**2,020**

**Number produced:
125 LD deriv.**
Jan/Nov	1956	21,281

**Number produced:
124 D deriv. 150**
May/Nov	1956	150

Frame numbering sequence from 150 D: 00.001

Frame numbering sequence from 150 LD: 105.001

Frame numbering sequence from 125 LD deriv.: 500.001

Identification details 150 D-LD

Version I 1954-mid-1955
Handlebar in aluminium, electrical system without battery and without current rectifier, 14 mm gudgeon pin, cylindrical power socket at flywheel, 3-notch gear shift, smooth starter casing (small bush on the cover of the last examples from mid-1955), silencer with chromed expansion box.

150 LD only: beige plastic air vent grilles on side panels.

Version II 1955-mid-1956
Electrical system with battery and rectifier, starter casing with three-screw cover, silencer with chromed expansion box, rear damper location (less inclined).

150 LD only: beige plastic air vent grilles on side panels.

Version III mid-1956 - end of production
Silencer without expansion box and with two brass inspection caps, 16 mm gudgeon pin, additional oil vent on final drive, quadrangular power socket at flywheel attached with a screw, control cables with lubricators at steeringhead, cylinder air manifold with central crest for the attachment screws, chromed steel handlebar, 5-notch gearshift, additional left-hand screw on the rear hub nut.

150 LD only: bump-stops with screws supporting the side panels, larger levers on the panels, side panel air vent grilles in chromed metal.

Identification details 125 LD deriv.

Version I to mid-1955
Silencer with chromed expansion box, beige plastic air vent grilles on side panels, 3-notch gearshift, floorboard runners with rubber inserts (as on the 150 LD), HT coil inside the flywheel magneto (earliest examples only).

Version II mid-1956 - end of production
Silencer without expansion box and with two brass inspection caps, side panel air vent grilles in chromed metal, 5-notch gearshift, chromed steel handlebar, control cables with lubricators, cylinder air manifold with central crest for the attachment screws.

Identification details 125 LD deriv. 150

Model destined for the Swiss market. In effect a 150 D reduced to 125 cc; the only aesthetic differences concern the elimination of the front 150D script. Engine specification identical to the 125 LD derivata.

Colour schemes and finishes 150D

Body colour parts
Fork, fork covers, frame, leg-shield, passenger grab-handle, fuel tank, glovebox and cover, 2 glovebox cross-members, headlamp, front and rear mudguards, wheel hubs, wheel rims, front brake shoe backing plate, front and rear saddle frames (including all the small springs), stand, 2 underfloor cross-members, spare wheel holder, license plate holder (painted in aluminium on the first 8,000 examples) and its bracket, torsion bar lever, cylinder head air intake manifold (4 pieces), upper part of damper, battery holder, round rectifier cover and its bracket, steeringhead badge mount.

Aluminium paint
Tool-carrier tube and its cover, license plate holder (first 8,000 examples only).

Crankcase (all castings) and intake manifold
Aluminium paint.

Carburettor
Air filter painted aluminium silver, burnished body, zinc-plated screws and fittings, float chamber in bare aluminium.

Control cable sheaths
Grey.

Saddles
Dark green imitation leather with "Innocenti" rear script.

Silencer
Matte black (in some cases the header is chromed, chrome-plated supplementary expansion chamber.

Colour schemes and finishes
150 LD and 125 deriv.

Body colour parts
Fork, fork covers, frame, leg-shield, fuel tank, headlamp bracket, front and rear mudguards, side-panels, wheel hubs, front brake shoe backing plate, front and rear saddle frames (including all the small springs), spare wheel holder, license plate holder (painted in aluminium on the first 8,000 examples) and its brackets, torsion bar lever, cylinder head air intake manifold (4 pieces), stand, upper part of damper, battery holder, round rectifier cover and its bracket, leg-shield internal glovebox (150 LD only).

Aluminium paint
Tool-carrier tube and its cover, license plate holder (first 8,000 examples only).

Crankcase
Aluminium paint (earliest examples only, successively bare aluminium).

Engine parts always painted aluminium
Air intake manifold, complete gear change casing.

Carburettor
Air filter painted aluminium silver, burnished body, zinc-plated screws and fittings, bare aluminium float chamber cover.

Control cable sheaths
Grey.

Saddles
Dark green, imitation leather with "Innocenti" rear script.

Silencer
Matte black, chromed supplementary expansion chamber.

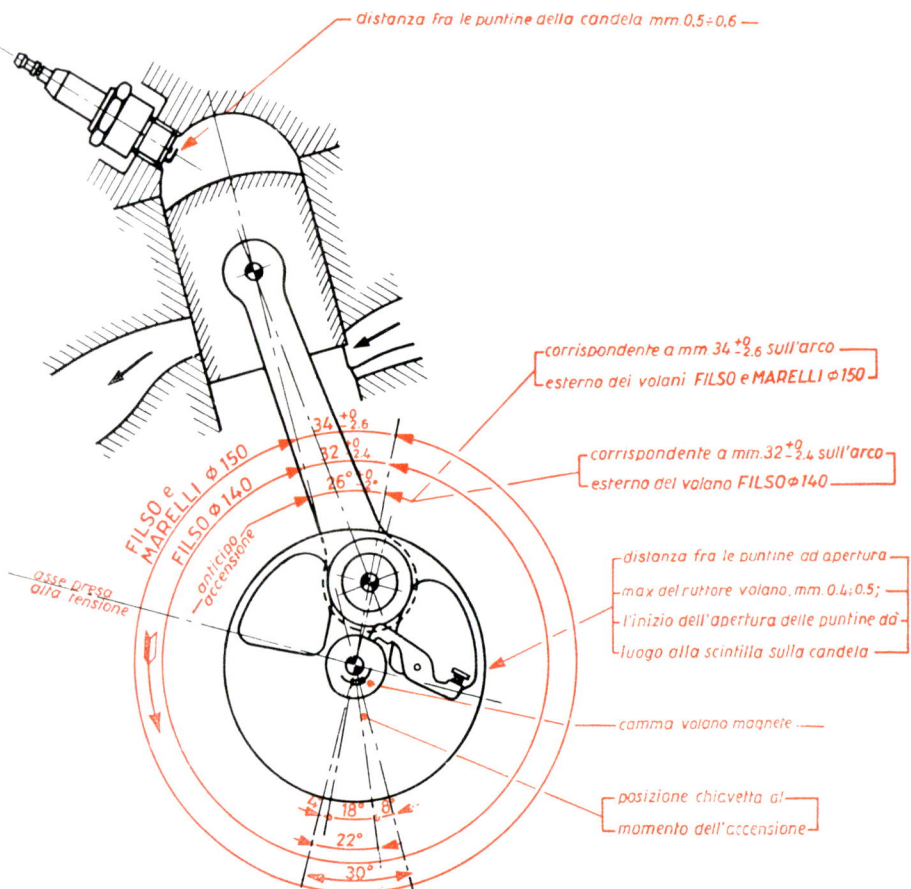

Chromed parts

Frame
Handlebar (if in steel) and its details, brake pedal, front saddle conical springs and rear saddle spring-tie-bar-cap, passenger footrest support rod, rear glovebox lock cover, steeringhead cable clip (150 D). Choke knob, steeringhead upper bearing support plate, side-panel grilles (125-150 LD). Speedometer bezel (150 LD).

Electrical parts
Headlamp and tail lamp surrounds, horn grille, light switch cover.

Engine
Kick-start pedal, supplementary expansion chamber.

Wheels
Large cap nuts (2 front, 1 rear).

Cadmium-plated parts

Front fork
Front wheel carriers, screws and pins.

Frame
All screws and bolts, torsion bar figure-of-eight clip, special washers, bushes.

Electrical parts
Light switch cover screws, horn stem and clip (150 D).

Engine
Levers, studs, screws.

Wheels
Nuts, bushes, wheel hub brake levers.

Attention: towards mid-1954 cadmium plating (similar to white zinc) was introduced in place of nickel plating. This new treatment was adopted once the stock of nickel-plated material was exhausted; it is therefore possible to find 1954-55 Lambrettas with both nickel- and plated-plated parts.

Above: instructions for perfect ignition timing.
Below: 3-position switch with separate horn button. This is the type commonly used on these models. Only on the earliest examples from the start of 1955 was a 3-position light switch with a chrome cover and an integrated horn button fitted (125 D-LD, late 1954).

Nickel-plated parts

Lubricator, oil caps, 14 mm wheel nuts, lower part of rear damper, steeringhead upper bush, fuel tap.

Burnished parts

Frame
Cap clip of the tool carrier tube.

Engine
Large and small Allen bolts, engine pivot, nut and washer.

Polished parts

Frame
Handlebar (if in aluminium), central clamp and lever carriers, floorboard runners, fuel tap lever. Side-panel levers, and floorboard runner ferrules (150 LD).

Engine
Kick-start lever (earliest examples of 150 LD, lever in aluminium).

Lechler system colours

Sand beige	8029
Light grey	8012
	(a number of 1956 examples only)
Aluminium (engine and frame)	Fiat 690

Maintenance data

Fuel/oil mixture:	6%
Spark plug:	Bosch 225 short thread
Engine oil:	SAE 15/50, 500 g
Final drive:	SAE 140 100 g.
Carburettor:	Dell'Orto MA 19B4 (150 cc), max jet 72, min 40 - Valve 75
Carburettor:	Dell'Orto MA 18B4, max jet 70, min 45 - Valve 75
Ignition advance:	24º - 26º 4 - 4.6 mm ahead of top dead centre

Upper photo: Exhaust with brass caps typical of the last version of the D-LD. This type, suitably modified, was also fitted to the first examples of the '57 LD.

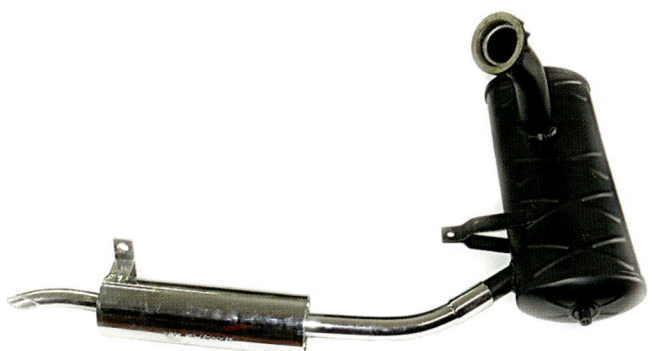

Middle photo: Exhaust with lateral covers and chromed expansion chamber fitted to both the versions I and II. On both models it is possible to find a chromed rather than exhaust header pipe.

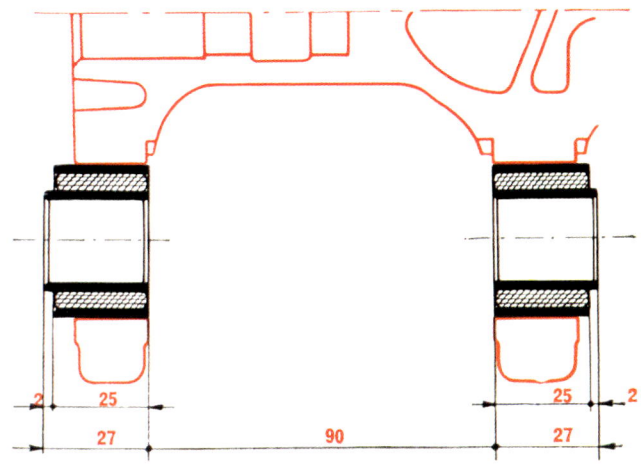

Crankcase silent block mounting diagram.

LAMBRETTA 125 - 150 LD 1957

Number produced:
125 LD '57

Dec	1956	1,030
Jan/Dec	1957	26,715
Jan/Jul	1958	16,920
Total		**44,665**

Number produced:
150 LD '57

Jan/Dec	1957	81,870
Jan/Jul	1955	31,983
Total:		**113,853**

Number produced:
125 '57 LD electric start

Mar/Jun	1957	52

Number produced:
150 LD '57 electric start

Apr/Dec	1957	4,076

Number produced: 150 LD "Inghilterra"

Dec '56/Jan '57	5,718

Frame numbering sequence from 125 LD '57: around 518,000

Frame numbering sequence from 150 LD '57: 200.001

Identification details 125-150 LD '57

Version I mid-May 1957
Insulating plates applied to inside wall of air filter box, front wheel hub without dust-trap labyrinth, silencer with 2 inspection ports and short tail-pipe, oil-lubricated starter mechanism, curved kick-start pedal.

125 only: dark green open-front saddle on the earliest examples, then as for the 150, black, closed-front.

Version II May 1957 - end of production
Filter box insulation plates eliminated, front hub with dust-trap labyrinth, silencer no longer opening and with tail-pipe extended through to rear brake, grease-lubricated starter mechanism, unified ball grease nipples, flat kick-start pedal, fuel tank with incorporated vent an fuel cap without breather hole, LI-type self-locking wheel nuts (last 1958 examples), front saddle frame with less pronounced spring mounts and with no runner protection on the bolts.

Identification details 150 LD special "Inghilterra"

Model produced on specific request for the British market: generally similar structure to the LD'57 but with the following variations: Leg-shield with horn below the headlamp, no handlebar fairing, control cable protection tubes, leg-shield internal glovebox with speedometer, special paintwork.

Colour schemes and finishes 150D

Body colour parts
Fork, fork covers, frame, leg-shield, fuel tank, front and rear mudguards, wheel hubs, wheel rims, front brake shoe backing plate, front and rear saddle frames (including all the small springs), spare wheel holder, stand, license plate holder and bracket, torsion bar lever, cylinder head air intake manifold (4 pieces), upper part of damper, tail-light body, rear glovebox lid, stand, battery holder, round rectifier cover and bracket (150 only), Speedometer plug cap (125 only), handlebar and central support (not for earliest examples). Headlamp surround, side-panels, body colour headset o the 125, different colour on 150.

Detail of the speedometer fitted as standard to the 150. The headlight "eyebrow" was instead a feature of both the 125 and the 150.

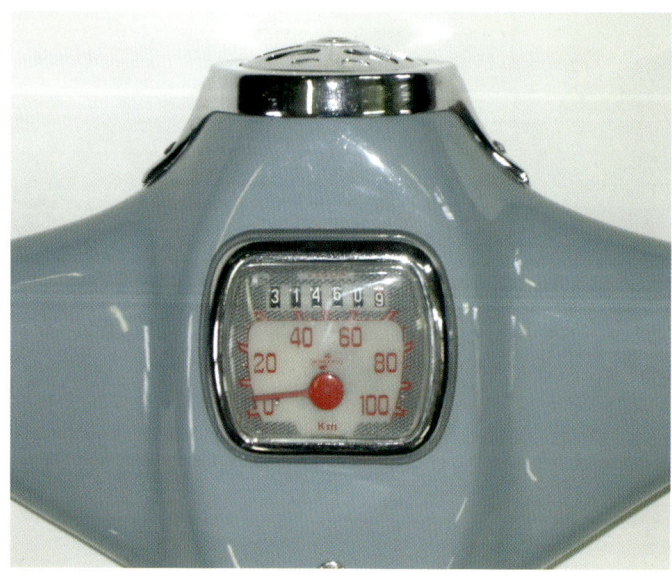

WIRING DIAGRAM

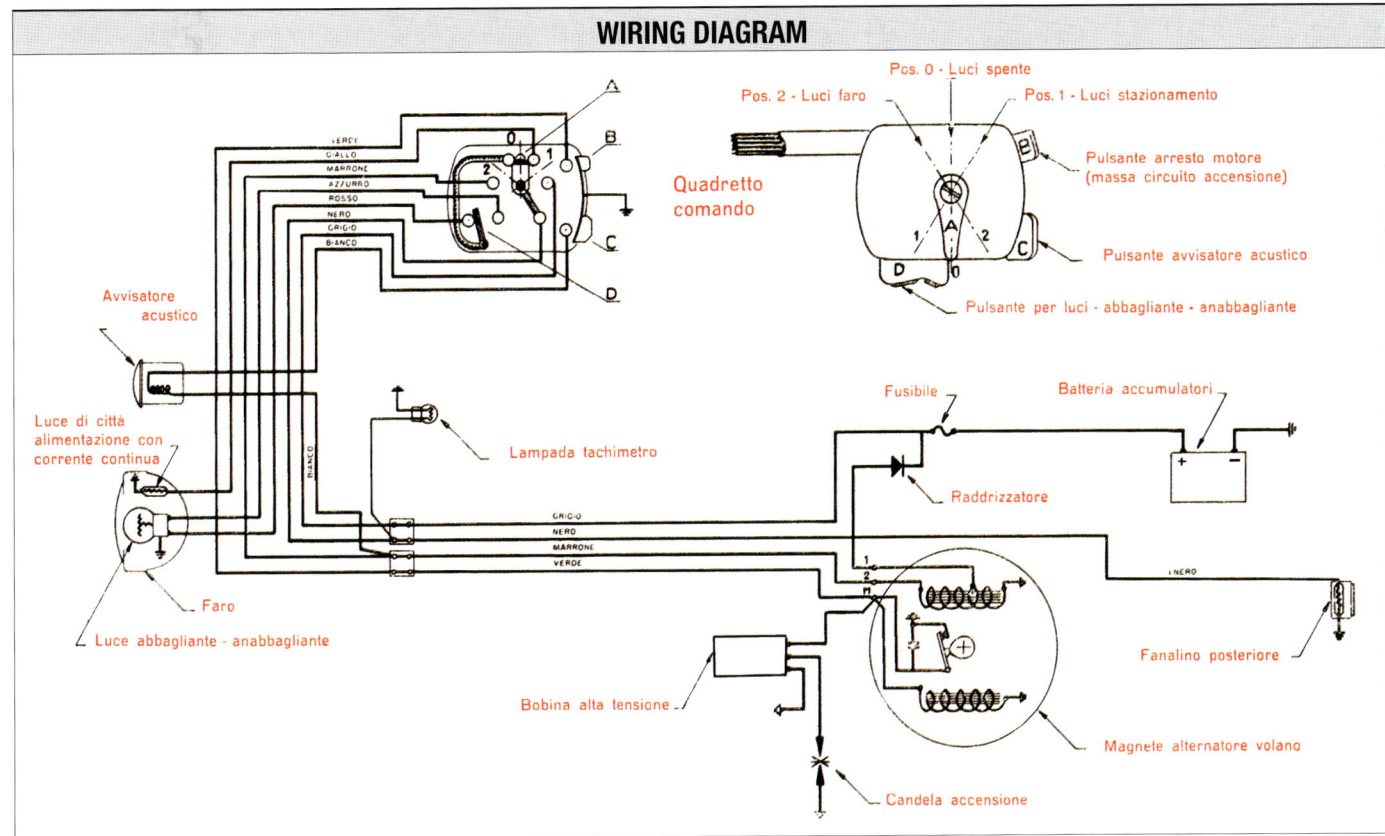

Crankcase
Bare aluminium.

Engine parts painted in aluminium
Intake manifold, gear-shift casing.

Carburettor
Air filter and float chamber cover bare aluminium, burnished body, zinc-plated screws and fittings.

Control cable sheaths
Grey.

Saddles
Black imitation leather with "Innocenti" rear script. Earliest 125 examples only 150 D-type dark green with "Innocenti" rear script.

Silencer
Matte black.

Chromed parts

Frame
Handlebar (earliest examples only) and its details, brake pedal, steeringhead cable clip, front saddle bi-conical springs and rear saddle spring-tie-bar-cap, choke knob, steeringhead upper bearing support plate, side-panel grilles, front "Lambretta LD" script, speedometer bezel (150).

Electrical parts
Headlamp bezel and ant-reflection eyebrow, bezel screws and washers, horn grille and bezel, light switch cover.

Wheels
Non-self-locking large cap nuts only (2 front, 1 rear).

Cadmium-plated parts

Front fork
Front wheel carriers, screws and pins, lower steeringhead bearing dust cap.

Frame
All screws and bolts, special washers, bushes.

EPICYCLIC KICK-START MECHANISM

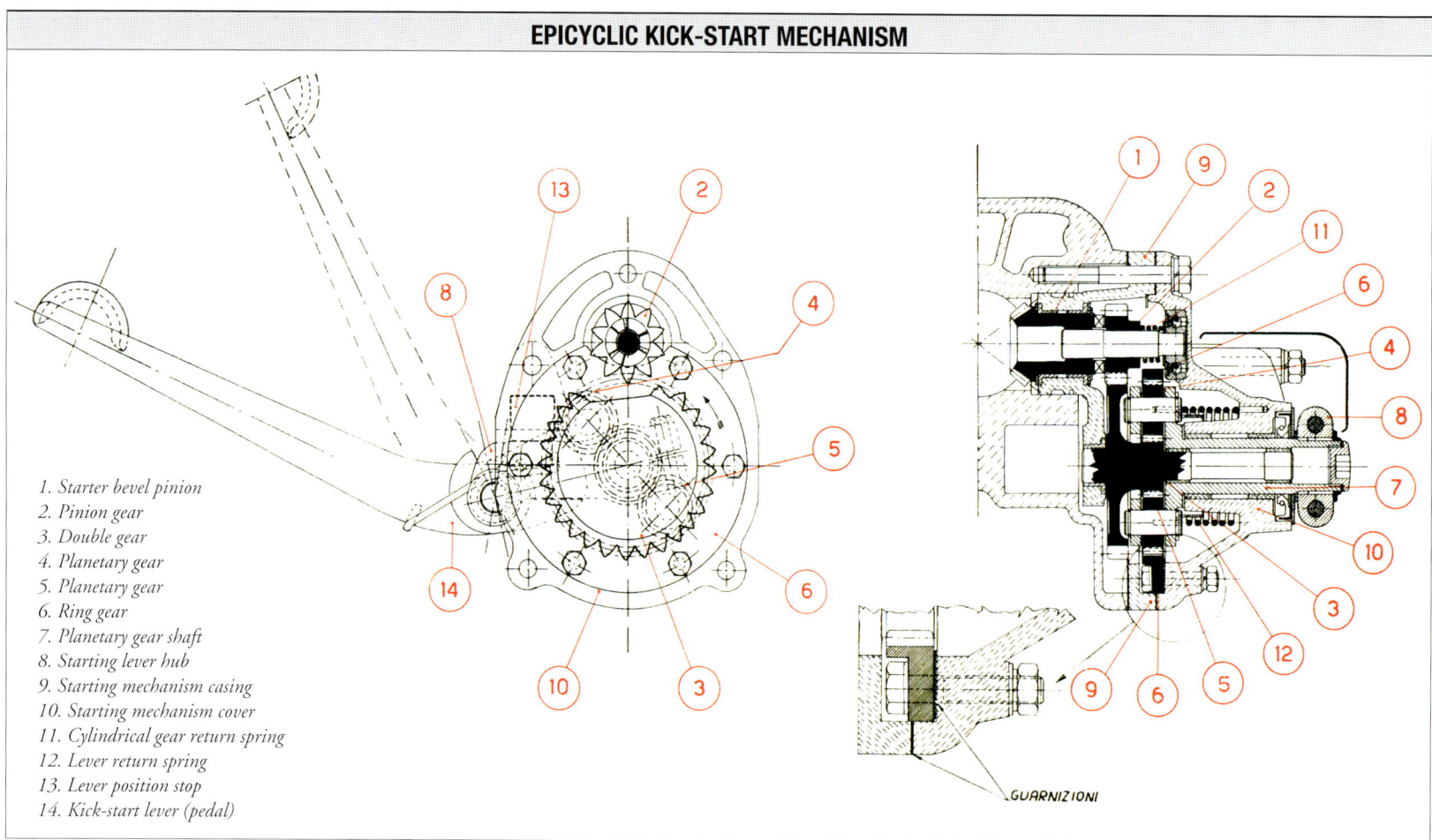

1. Starter bevel pinion
2. Pinion gear
3. Double gear
4. Planetary gear
5. Planetary gear
6. Ring gear
7. Planetary gear shaft
8. Starting lever hub
9. Starting mechanism casing
10. Starting mechanism cover
11. Cylindrical gear return spring
12. Lever return spring
13. Lever position stop
14. Kick-start lever (pedal)

Engine
Levers, studs, screws.

Wheels
Open and cap nuts, bushes, wheel hub brake levers, large wheel hub nuts (2 front, 1 rear, self-locking type only).

Nickel-plated parts

Lubricators, oil caps, lower part of rear damper (150), light switch cover screws.

Burnished parts

Engine
Large and small Allen bolts, cast-iron kick-start lever support hub, engine pivot.

Frame
Torsion bar figure-of-eight clip.

Polished parts

Frame
Handlebar lever carriers, floorboard runners and ferrules central clamp and lever carriers, fuel tap lever, side-panel levers.

Engine
Kick-start lever.

Lechler system colours

125 LD
Earth grey   8041, single colour for all bodywork

150 LD
Earth grey   8041 for all bodywork except
                      side-panels, headset and headlamp
                      surround which may be:

Maroon   8020
Emerald green   8051
England blue   8031
Tirreno Brasil C blue
(Fiat)   0401

Maintenance data

Fuel/oil mixture: 6%
Spark plug: Bosch 225 short thread
Engine oil: SAE 15/50, 540 g
Final drive: SAE 140 100 g.
Carburettor: Dell'Orto MA 19B4 (150 cc),
                      max jet 75, min - 40 Valve 75
Carburettor: Dell'Orto MA 18B4 (125 cc),
                      max jet 70, min - 45 Valve 75
Ignition advance: 24° - 26° 4 - 4.6 mm
                      ahead of top dead centre

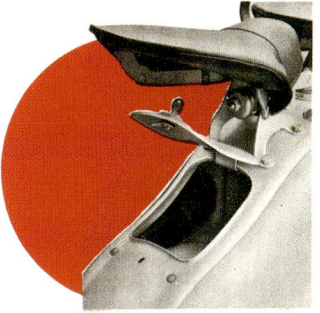

On the 1957 Lambretta, the glovebox has found new home so attractive and elegant that it may be defined as "natural". A spacious and highly convenient compartment has been created in the central rib of the fairing, immediately below the rear saddle where it does nothing to interfere with the styling.

Among the new features with which the 1957 Lambretta made its bow, one of the most welcome will be that of the new intake system and the new exhaust silencer. The result of these changes will be a very attractive exhaust note.

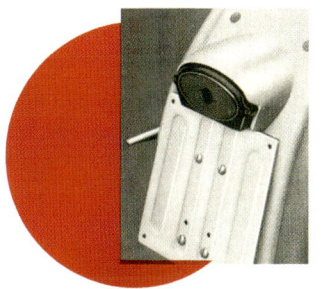

This is how the new taillight on the latest 1957 Lambretta LD looks. Elegantly styled and perfectly integrated with the fairing, the new tail-light is also more efficient.

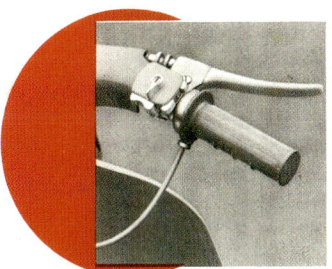

The 1957 model Lambretta is equipped with elegantly styled and perfectly efficient new electrical switchgear. The convenience of the controls of this new switch is the fruit of experience.

The handlebar of the 1957 Lambretta has been fully faired in such a way that the internal cable runs and the central location of the illuminated speedometer and the horn lend the component a soberly elegant appearance.

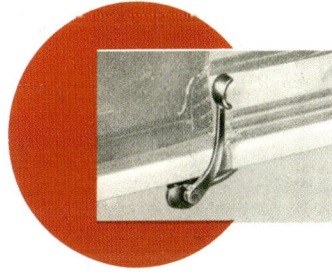

The 1957 Lambretta LD 150 benefits from a new starting system. The promptness and ease of the new system will be a pleasant surprise, especially our fairer clients (ladies and girls).

Number produced: 175 TV	
Sep/Dec 1957	1,125
Jan/Dec 1958	8,961
Total	**10,086**

Frame numbering sequence from 175 TV: 1.001

LAMBRETTA 175 TV

Identification details 175 TV

First version to April 1958
Headlamp cowl with integrated horn grille (non-removable), flywheel side ball bearings.

First 1800 examples only: brake-clutch control regulators functioning, subsequently locked with a pin.

Second version May 1958 - July 1958
Removable headlamp cowl with integrated horn grille, flywheel side roller bearings, stand mudguard, additional locking washer on rear wheel nut.

Third version- to end of production
Brake-clutch control regulators eliminated, additional rubber protection on rear brake cable.

Colour schemes and finishes 175 TV

Body colour parts
Fork, frame, leg-shield, fuel tank, rear floorboards, front and rear mudguards, headlamp cowling (and horn grille versions II and III), side-panels, handlebar and headset, floorboard tunnel, wheel hubs, Front brake shoe backing plate, saddle frame and fixing plate, spare wheel holder, cylinder head air intake manifold (4 pieces), 1 rear and 2 front dampers, tail-light body, glovebox lid, stand, battery holder, round rectifier cover and bracket, carburettor intake duct, stand mudguard (versions II and III), rear air intake grille fins.

Wheel rims
Version I painted only on the side of the wheel nuts, the rest chromed, versions II and III, the painted part reaches the curve of the shoulder and only the border of the shoulder is chromed.

Attention: the rear mudguard, the cylinder cap, the lower sides of the passenger running boards and the central floorboard and the insides of the side panels were coated with anti-noise black paint before being finished in the body colour.

Crankcase
Bare aluminium.

Carburettor
Carburettor body, air filter and float chamber cover bare aluminium, zinc-plated air filter cover, screws and fittings.

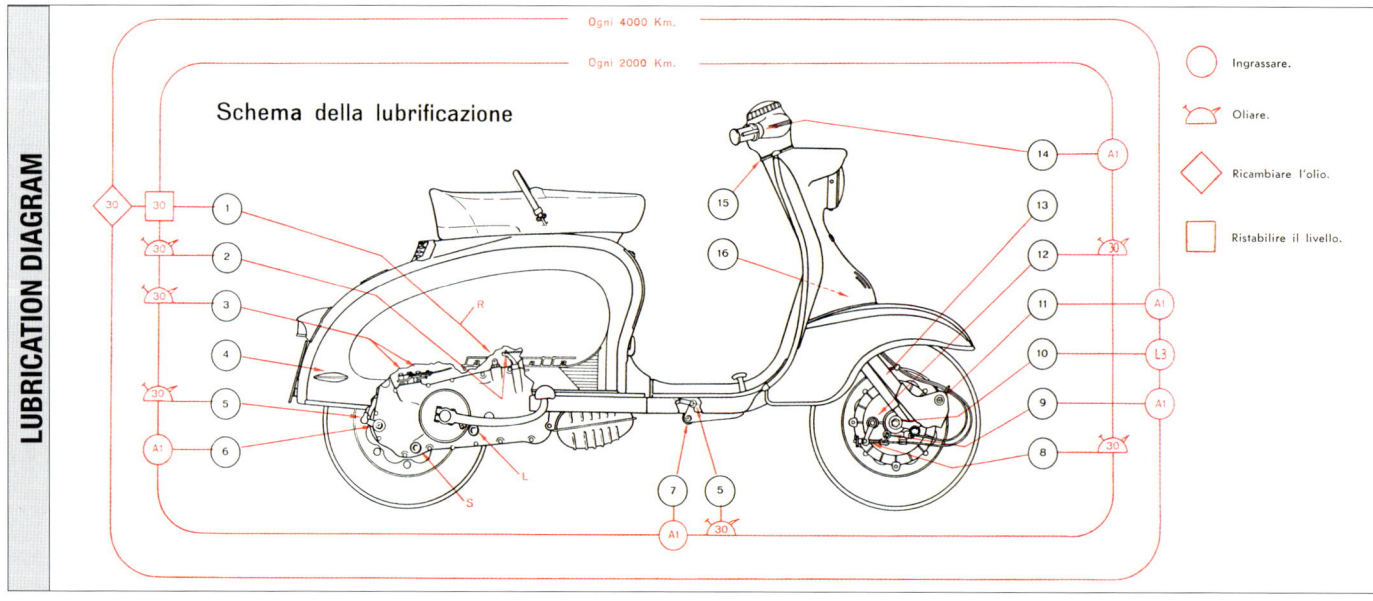

Top: on the left, a detail of the wheel rim colour for the version I, on the right, the version II and III.

Control cable sheaths
Grey.

Saddles
Black imitation leather with "Innocenti" rear script.

Silencer
Black.

Chromed parts

Frame
Rear brake pedal, handlebar adjusters, threaded kick-start lever bush, steering lock cover, ring below handlebars, all scripts on leg-shield and side-panels, lower steeringhead bearing cap, glovebox lid lock. Front suspension wheel carriers (rough chromed).

Electrical parts
Headlamp bezel, bezel screws and washers, ignition lock bezel and cover.

Engine
Kick-start lever and spring cover.

Wheels
Rims (part painted).

Cadmium-plated parts

Front fork
Screws and pins.

Frame
All screws and bolts, special washers, bushes.

Engine
Levers, studs, screws.

Wheels
Plain and cap nuts, bushes, wheel hub brake levers.

Nickel-plated parts

Lubricators, oil caps.

Burnished parts

Engine
Engine pivot.

Polished parts

Frame
Handlebar levers and carriers, fuel tap and choke levers, side-panel levers, speedometer bezel, leg shield profile terminals, rear air intake grill (external part only).

Electrical parts
Handlebar light switch cover.

Lechler system colours

Ivory   8028

Maintenance data

Fuel/oil mixture: 6%
Spark plug: Bosch 225/240 long thread
Engine oil: SAE 30, 1,000 cc
Final drive: SAE 140 100 g.
Carburettor: Dell'Orto MA 23BS5
                     max jet 105, min 40 - Valve 70
Ignition advance: 24° - 28° 32-33 mm
                     on flywheel circumference

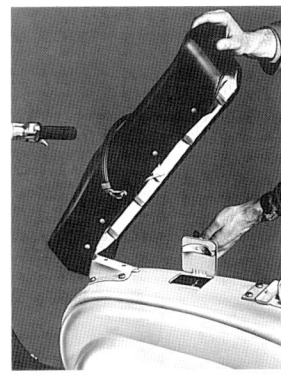

The long saddle of the TV with the unusual painting of the frame in the same colour as the bodywork.

LAMBRETTA 125-150 LI

Number produced: 150 LI
Apr/Dec 1958   41,924
Jan/Oct 1959   67,060
Total   108,984

Number produced: 125 LI
Jun/Dec 1958   20,809
Jan/Oct 1959   26,938
Total   47,747

Frame numbering sequence from 150 LI:
500.001

Frame numbering sequence from 125 LI:
500.001

Identification details 125-150 LI

Version I to September 1958
Oval air intakes at the base of the side-panels (early examples through to June 1958), fixed, non-adjustable chain tensioner guides, air filter with metal mesh with air intake beneath the rear saddle, passenger grab handle on rear saddle.

125 LI only: earliest examples without leg-shield rubber profile trim and without steering lock.

Version II September 1958 - December 1958
Adjustable chain tensioner guides, cylindrical supplementary filter with paper element, passenger grab handle on front saddle, additional dust protection bellows on rear brake cable.

Version III December 1958 - to end of production
New induction system with oval filter and air intake beneath the front saddle, shorter exhaust tail-pipe collar, rear brake pedal with small spray guard.

Final variants to March 1959
Fuel cap with incorporated breather, double threaded removable wheel hub studs. Front brake cable moved outside the fork (modification from July 1959).

Colour schemes 150 LI

Body colour parts
Fork, frame, leg-shield, fuel tank, rear floorboards, front mudguard inside and outside, rear mudguard, floorboard tunnel, wheel hubs, front brake shoe backing plate, wheel rims, saddle frame and large central springs, spare wheel holder, cylinder head air intake manifold (2 pieces), glovebox and lid, tail-light body, fuel tap hatch, stand, stand mudguard, battery holder, round rectifier cover and bracket, right-hand rear floorboard L-bracket, license plate holder. Carburettor intake duct (Version I only). Intake manifold, filter holder and air intake beneath saddle (Version III only). If the base colour is River Grey (especially the earliest examples with the oval side-panel air intakes) the headlamp cowling, the horn grille, the handlebar and headset and the side-panels are painted in the same colour. If instead the base colour is Dawn Grey, these elements may be painted in the following colour variants: Flaminia Blue, England Blue, Nile Green, Ruby Red, Coral Red.

Colour schemes 125 LI

Body colour parts (Dawn Grey only)
Fork, frame, leg-shield, headlamp cowling, horn grille, rear floorboards, handlebar and headset, speedometer plug, handlebar lever carriers, rear air intake grille, fuel tank, front mudguard inside and outside, rear mudguard, floorboard tunnel, wheel hubs, front brake shoe backing plate, saddle frame and large central springs, spare wheel holder, cylinder head air intake manifold (2 pieces), tail-light body, glovebox lid, fuel tap hatch, stand, stand mudguard, glovebox, right-hand rear floorboard L-bracket. Carburettor intake duct (Version I only). Intake manifold, filter holder and air intake beneath saddle (Version III only). The side-panels only are painted dark Steel Grey, license plate holder.

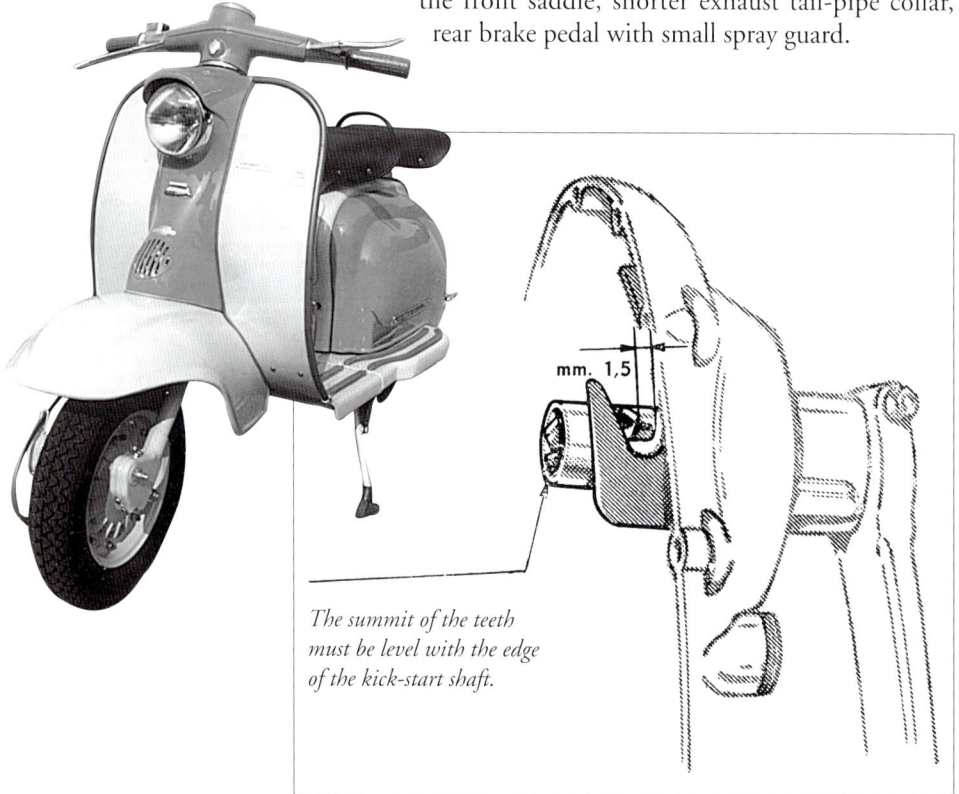

The summit of the teeth must be level with the edge of the kick-start shaft.

Finishes 125-150 LI

Black finish
Rear damper

Crankcase
Bare aluminium.

Carburettor
Carburettor body, air filter and float chamber cover bare aluminium, zinc-plated screws and fittings. Cylindrical supplementary filter box (Version II) painted black.

Control cable sheaths
Grey.

Saddles
Black imitation leather with "Innocenti" rear script.

Silencer
Matte black.

Chromed parts

Frame
Brake pedal, frame tube cable circlip, "Lambretta LI" script on leg-shield, ring beneath steeringhead, threaded kick-start lever bush, glovebox lock.

Electrical parts
Headlamp bezel, right-hand light switch screws and cover.

Engine
Kick-start lever.

Cadmium-plated parts

Front fork
Screws and pins, lower steeringhead bearing dust cap, wheel carriers.

Frame
All screws and bolts, special washers, bushes. Tie bars, pins and nuts for horizontal saddle frame springs, stand fixing plates, rear brake pedal removable spray guard.

Engine
Levers, studs, screws and nuts.

Wheels
Plain and cap nuts, bushes, wheel hub brake levers.

Electrical parts
Rectifier cover (150 LI). In some cases it may be black.

Nickel-plated parts

Lubricators, oil caps.

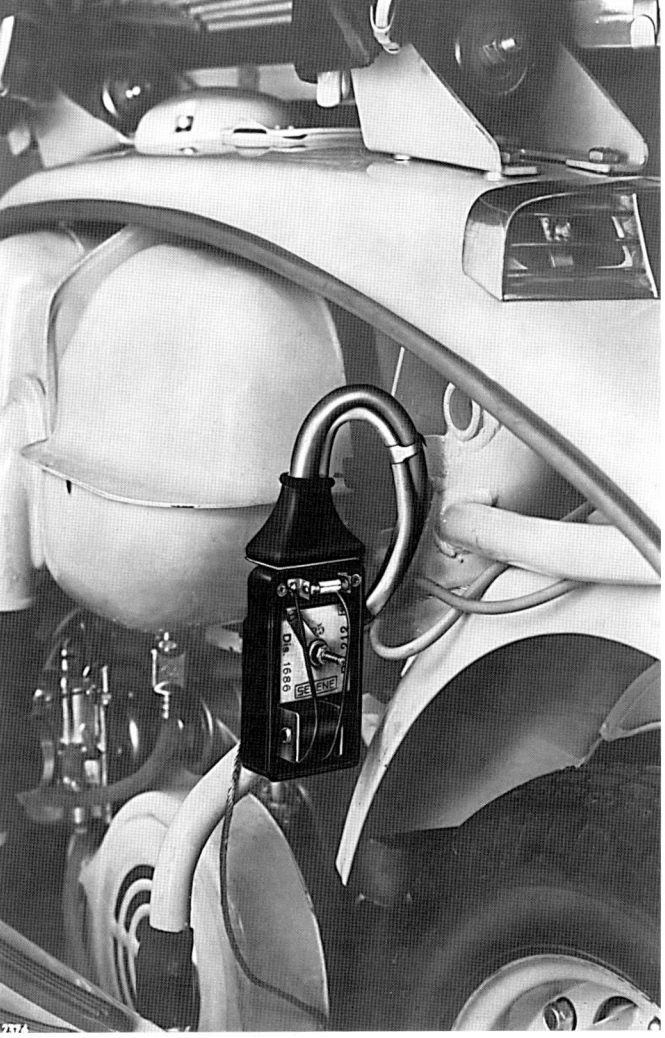

Detail of the current rectifier mounted on those models equipped with a battery. Note that the air intake under the saddle is fitted without a rubber seal.

Opposite page: diagram of the adjustment of the slide moving the kick-start piston. Applicable to the LI-TV-S models through to 1967.

150 LI - DIAGRAM OF ELECTRICAL SYSTEM (PRE-MODIFICATION)

1. *Speedometer lamp*
2. *Headlight*
3. *Electric horn*
4. *Ignition off button*
5. *Switchgear with light switch*
6. *Junction box*
7. *Battery*
8. *Rectifier*
9. *HT coil*
10. *Tail light*
11. *Spark plug mount*
12. *Flywheel magneto power outlet*
13. *Impedance and fuse*

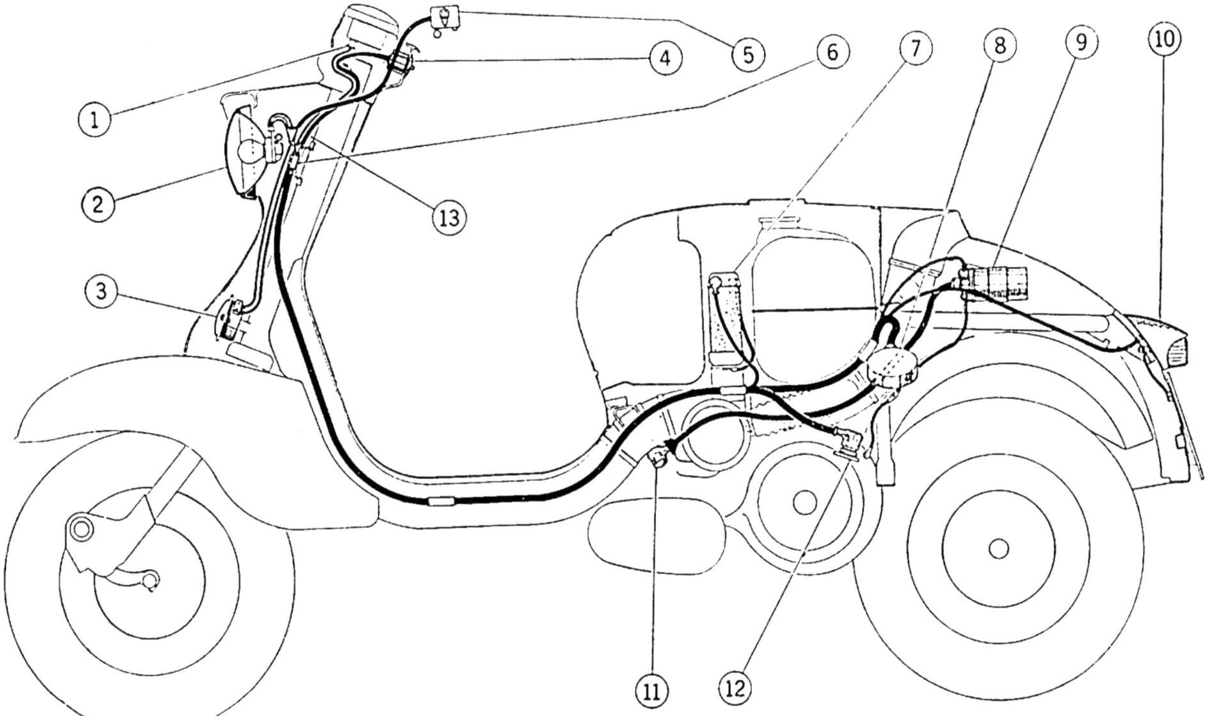

Burnished parts

Frame
Stand spring, brake pedal spring, fuel tank support straps.

Polished parts

Frame
Fuel tap and choke levers, handlebar levers, side-panel levers, speedometer bezel, Lambretta script on side-panels, floorboard runners, leg shield profile terminals.

150 LI only: handlebar lever carriers, rear air intake grill, floorboard runner ferrules.

Electrical parts
Handlebar Off switch.

Lechler system colours

125 LI
Dawn Grey	8019
Dark Steel Grey	8040 (125 side-panels only)

150 LI
River Grey	8014 (single-colour bodywork)
Dawn Grey	8019 (two-tone bodywork)

For the side-panels, the headlamp cowling, horn grille, handlebar and headset:

Flaminia Blue	8032
England Blue	8031
Nile Green	8015
Ruby Red	8047
Coral Red	8046

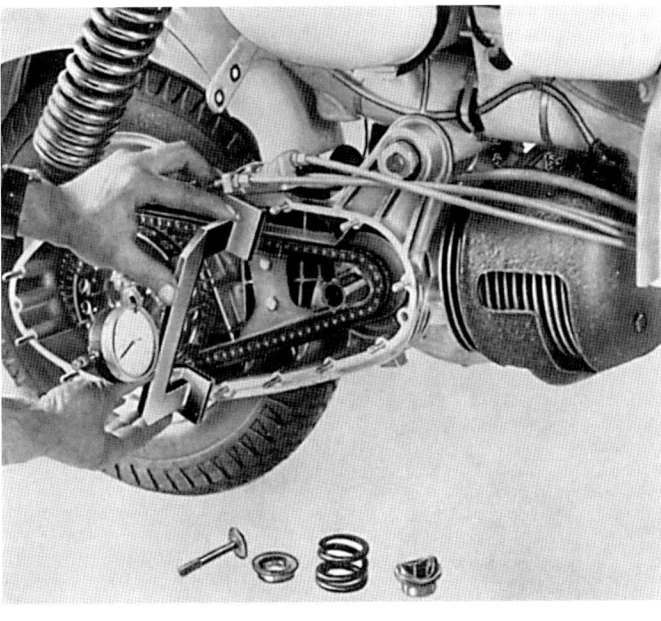

Tool for checking that the chain is parallel. This operation is necessary when, for example, the sprocket and the crown wheel are changed.

Maintenance data

Fuel/oil mixture:	4%
Spark plug:	Bosch 225/240 long thread
Engine oil:	SAE 90, 600 cc
Carburettor (150 LI):	Dell'Orto MA 19BS5 max jet 96, min 40 - Valve 65
Carburettor (125 LI):	Dell'Orto MA 18BS5 max jet 93, min 35 - Valve 50
Ignition advance:	22° - 24° 32-33 mm on flywheel circumference

LAMBRETTA 175 TV SERIES II

Number produced:

Frame number 100.000

| Jan/Oct | 1959 | 8,772 |

Frame number 200.000

Oct/Dec	1959	3,260
Jan/Dec	1960	19,456
Jan/Nov	1961	12,212
Total		43,700

First version frame numbering sequence from: 100.001

Second version frame numbering sequence from: 200.001

Cutaway exhibition engine; note the finishing of the cylinder cover with anti-noise and normal paint.

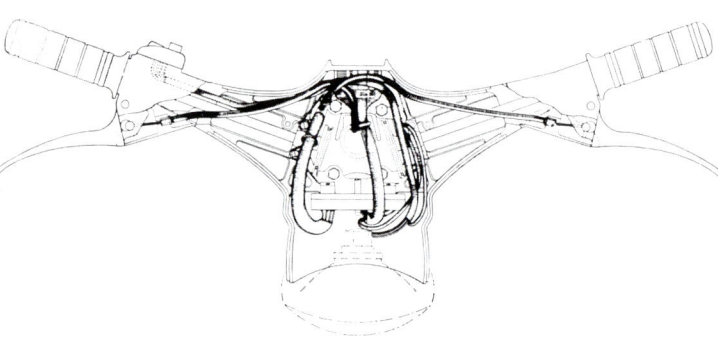

Identification details

First version to October 1959 (100.000)
Frame with longitudinal rib welded along the centreline of the tube, 23 mm carburettor, small tail light (142x43 mm), round, grey horn grille, air filter pipe fixed with a screw clamp, stand mudguard attached with 8 5 mm bolts, flywheel side bearing lubricated by the petroil mixture. Short piston (earliest examples only).

Second version (200.000) to mid-1960
Frame with normal tube without welding, 21 mm carburettor, flywheel side bearing lubricated with grease, long piston, large tail light (130x58 mm), round, grey horn grille, air filter pipe fixed with a screw clamp.

Second version from mid-1960 to January 1961
Stand mudguard fixed with two 8 mm bolts (from October 1960), round, grey horn grille, air filter pipe fixed with a screw clamp.

Second version from February 1961 to end of production
Air filter pipe fixed with a spring clip, larger air filter (version III type).

Colour schemes and finishes

Body colour parts
Fork, frame, leg-shield, fuel tank, rear floorboards, handle-bar and headset, side-panels, headlamp cowling, horn grille, inside and outside of front mudguard, rear mudguard, floorboard tunnel, wheel hubs, front brake shoe backing plate, wheel rims, spare wheel holder, cylinder head air intake manifold (2 pieces), glovebox and lid, tail-light body, fuel tap hatch, stand, stand mudguard, right-hand rear running-board L-bracket, battery holder and strap, air box, filter carrier and air intake beneath the saddle, front dampers, license plate holder.

Attention: the rear mudguard, half of the cylinder cap (the sparkplug part), the lower edges of the passenger running boards and the central floorboard were coated with sound-deadening black paint. The insides of the side panels before being finished in the body colour were coated with sound-deadening black paint.

Black finish
Rear damper, saddle frame and clamp.

Crankcase
Bare aluminium.

Carburettor
Carburettor body and float chamber cover bare aluminium, zinc-plated, screws and fittings.

Control cable sheaths
Grey.

Saddles
Black imitation leather with "Innocenti" rear script.

Silencer
Matte black.

Chromed parts

Frame
Brake pedal, frame tube cable clip, "Lambretta 175 TV" script on leg-shield and side-panels, ring below handlebars, threaded kick-start lever bush.

Electrical parts
Headlamp bezel, right-hand light switch screws, ignition lock bezel and cover.

Engine
Kick-start lever.

Wheels
Front wheel carriers (rough chromed without polishing).

Cadmium-plated parts

Cadmium-plated parts

Front fork
Screws and pins, lower steeringhead bearing dust cap.

Frame
All screws and bolts, special washers, bushes. Stand mounting plates (through to mid-1960).

Electrical parts
Rectifier box cover (may be painted gloss black in some cases).

Engine
Levers, studs, nuts and bolts.

Wheels
Plain and cap nuts, bushes, wheel hub brake levers.

Nickel-plated parts

Lubricators, oil caps.

Burnished parts

Engine
Air filter pipe fixing spring (IV version only from Feb. 1961).

Frame
Stand spring, brake pedal spring, fuel tank support strap.

Polished parts

Frame
Fuel tap and choke levers, side-panel levers, floorboard runners and ferrules, leg shield profile terminals, handlebar lever carriers, rear grille, glovebox lock lever.

Electrical parts
Handlebar light switch cover.

Lechler system colours

Tyrrhenian Blue	8028
Oriental Yellow	8049

CYLINDER AND PISTON ASSEMBLY TOLERANCES AND WEAR LIMITS

TIPO	Selezione	MONTAGGIO NORMALE				1ª MAGGIORAZIONE				2ª MAGGIORAZIONE				3ª MAGGIORAZIONE				Gioco al Montagg.	Gioco al limite di usura
		CILINDRO		PISTONE		CILINDRO		PISTONE		CILINDRO		PISTONE		CILINDRO		PISTONE			
		R.cambio N.	ø C Toll.	Ricambio N.	ø C Toll.	Ricambio N.	ø C Toll.	Ricambio N.	ø B Toll.	R.cambio N.	ø C Toll.	Ricambio N.	ø B Toll.	R.cambio N.	ø C Toll.	Ricambio N.	ø B Toll.	D	D
125 li	0 / +	19111020/	52,0 +0/+0,006 +0,007/+0,013 +0,014/+0,020	19112150/	51,9 +0,060/+0,066 +0,067/+0,073 +0,074/+0,080	19112160/	52,1 +0/+0,006 +0,007/+0,013 +0,014/+0,020		52,4 +0,060/+0,066 +0,067/+0,073 +0,074/+0,080	19112170/	52,3 +0/+0,006 +0,007/+0,013 +0,014/+0,020		52,6 +0,060/+0,066 +0,067/+0,073 +0,074/+0,080	19112180/	52,5 +0/+0,006 +0,007/+0,013 +0,014/+0,020		+0,060/+0,066 +0,067/+0,073 +0,074/+0,080	Min. D=0,034 Max D=0,046	D=0,15
150 li	0 / +	19011020/	57,0 +0/+0,006 +0,007/+0,013 +0,014/+0,020	19012150/	56,9 +0,056/+0,062 +0,063/+0,069 +0,070/+0,076	19012160/	57,1 +0/+0,006 +0,007/+0,013 +0,014/+0,020		57,2 +0,056/+0,062 +0,063/+0,069 +0,070/+0,076	19012170/	57,3 +0/+0,006 +0,007/+0,013 +0,014/+0,020		57,4 +0,056/+0,062 +0,063/+0,069 +0,070/+0,076	19012180/	57,5 +0/+0,006 +0,007/+0,013 +0,014/+0,020		+0,056/+0,062 +0,063/+0,069 +0,070/+0,076	Min. D=0,038 Max D=0,050	D=0,15
175 Tv	0 / +	19211020/	62,0 +0/+0,006 +0,007/+0,013 +0,014/+0,020	19212090/	61,9 +0,050/+0,056 +0,057/+0,063 +0,064/+0,070	19212100/	62,1 +0/+0,006 +0,007/+0,013 +0,014/+0,020		62,2 +0,050/+0,056 +0,057/+0,063 +0,064/+0,070	19212110/	62,3 +0/+0,006 +0,007/+0,013 +0,014/+0,020		62,4 +0,050/+0,056 +0,057/+0,063 +0,064/+0,070	19212120/	62,5 +0/+0,006 +0,007/+0,013 +0,014/+0,020		+0,050/+0,056 +0,057/+0,063 +0,064/+0,070	Min. D=0,044 Max D=0,056	D=0,15

Maintenance data

Fuel/oil mixture:	4%
Spark plug:	Bosch 225/240 long thread
Engine oil:	SAE 90, 600 cc
Carburettor (1st version):	Dell'Orto MA 23BS5 max jet 110, min 40 - Valve 70
Carburettor (2nd version):	Dell'Orto MA 21BS5/BS7 max jet 88, min 40 - Valve 70
Ignition advance:	22º - 24º 32-33 mm on flywheel circumference

Above: this table of tolerances and wear limits is also applicable to the version III LI and TV. Bottom photo: the 6-volt battery fitted to the 150 LI II and the 175 TV II. The battery powered the position lights, brake lit and horn.

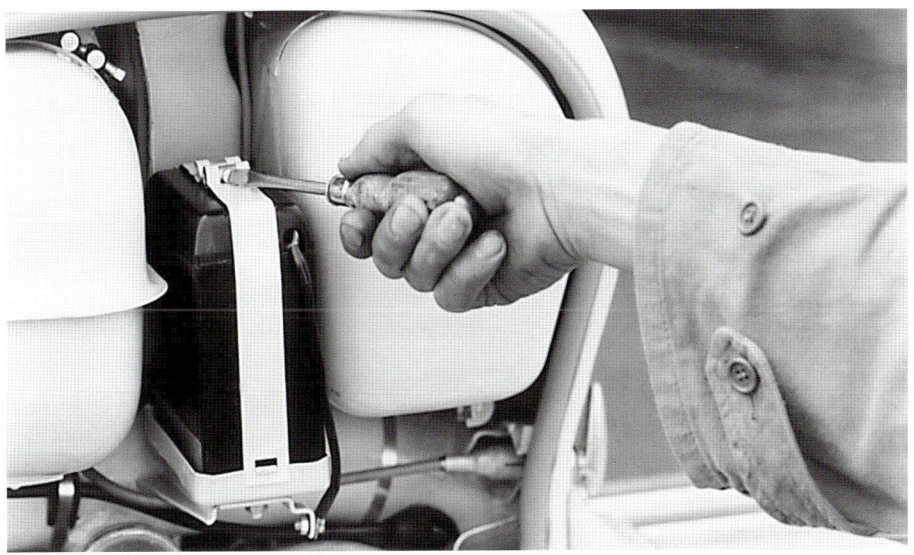

LAMBRETTA 125-150 LI SERIES II

Number produced:
125 LI II

Oct/Dec	1958	9,838
Jan/Dec	1959	59,221
Total		**111,087**

Number produced:
150 LI II

Oct/Dec	1959	23,645
Jan/Dec	1960	82,539
Jan/Nov	1961	55,856
Total		**162,040**

Frame numbering sequence from 125 LI:
700.001.
Last batch: 300.001

Frame numbering sequence from 150 LI:
800.001

Identification details 125-150 LI

Version I to mid-1960
Small rear light (142x43), round horn grille, air filter pipe fixed with screw clamp, stand mudguard fixed with eight 5 mm bolts.

Version II mid-1960 - January 1961
Large rear light (130x58 mm), oval horn grille, air filter pipe fixed with screw clamp, stand mudguard fixed with two 8 mm bolts (from October 1960).

Version III from February 1961 to end of production
Air filter pipe with spring clip, larger air filter (version III type).

Colour schemes 150 LI

150 LI
Body colour parts
Fork, frame, leg-shield, fuel tank, rear floorboards, handlebar and headset, front mudguard inside and outside, rear mudguard, floorboard tunnel, wheel hubs, front brake shoe backing plate, wheel rims, saddle frames and large central springs, spare wheel holder, cylinder head air intake manifold (2 pieces), glovebox and lid, tail-light body, fuel tap hatch, stand, stand mudguard, battery holder, air box, right-hand rear floorboard L-bracket, filter carrier and air intake beneath saddle, license plate holder. The headlamp cowling, the horn grille and the side-panels are painted in the following colour variants: Flaminia Blue, England Blue, Nile Green, Ruby Red, Coral Red. It is also possible to paint only the side-panels in the contrasting colour and leave the front cowling and horn grille in the body colour.

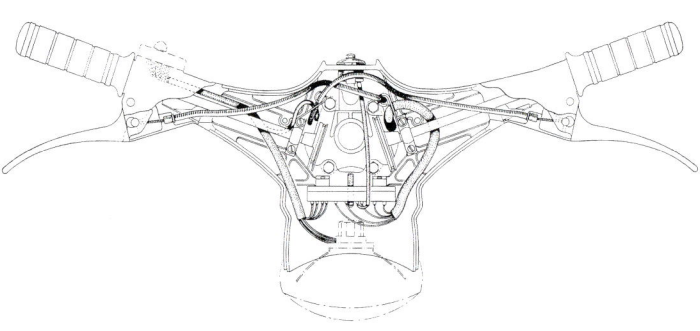

Colour schemes 125 LI

125 LI
Body colour parts
Fork, frame, leg-shield, headlamp cowling, rear floorboards, horn grille, handlebar and headset, handlebar lever carriers, rear air intake grille, fuel tank, front mudguard inside and outside, rear mudguard, floorboard tunnel, wheel hubs, front brake shoe backing plate, wheel rims, saddle frames and large central springs, spare wheel holder, cylinder head air intake manifold (2 pieces), glovebox and lid, tail-light body, fuel tap hatch, stand, stand mudguard, air box, right-hand rear floorboard L-bracket, filter holder pipe and air intake beneath saddle (Version III only), license plate holder. The side-panels only are painted dark Steel Grey.

Finishes 125-150 LI

Black finish
Rear damper

Crankcase
Bare aluminium.

Carburettor
Carburettor body and float chamber cover bare aluminium, zinc-plated screws and fittings.

Control cable sheaths
Grey.

Saddles
Black imitation leather with "Innocenti" rear script.

Silencer
Matte black.

Chromed parts:

Frame
Brake pedal, frame tube cable circlip, "Lambretta LI" script on legshield, ring beneath steeringhead, threaded kick-start lever bush.

Electrical parts
Headlamp bezel, right-hand light switch screws and cover.

Engine
Kick-start lever.

Front fork
Screws and pins, lower steeringhead bearing dust cap, wheel carriers.

Frame
All screws and bolts, special washers, bushes. Tie bars, pins and nuts for horizontal saddle frame springs, stand fixing plates (version III only).

Electrical parts
Rectifier box (150 LI).

Engine
Levers, studs, screws and nuts.

Wheels
Plain and cap nuts, bushes, wheel hub brake levers.

Nickel-plated parts

Lubricators, oil caps.

Burnished parts

Engine
Air filter pipe fixing spring (version III only).

Frame
Stand spring, brake pedal spring, fuel tank support straps.

Polished parts

Frame
Fuel tap and choke levers, side-panel levers, handlebar levers, Lambretta script on side-panels, floorboard runners, leg shield profile terminals, glovebox lock lever.
150 LI only: handlebar lever carriers, rear air intake grill, floorboard runner ferrules.

Electrical parts
Handlebar Off switch.

Lechler system colours

125 LI
Dawn Grey	8019
Dark Steel Grey	8040 (side-panels only)

150 LI
Dawn Grey	8019
River Grey	8014 (certain 1st version examples only)
Whitethorn	8082 (certain late 2nd 2nd version examples only)

For the side-panels, the headlamp cowling, horn grille, handlebar and headset:

Flaminia Blue	8032
England Blue	8031
Nile Green	8015
Ruby Red	8047
Coral Red	8046

Maintenance data

Fuel/oil mixture:	2%
Spark plug:	Bosch 225/240 long thread
Engine oil:	SAE 90, 600 cc
Carburettor (125 LI):	Dell'Orto MA 18BS5/BS7 max jet 73, min 35 - Valve 50
Carburettor (150 LI):	Dell'Orto MA 19BS5/BS7 max jet 78, min 40 - Valve 50
Ignition advance:	22º - 24º 32-33 mm on flywheel circumference

Demonstration of the tool for compressing the springs and facilitating the removal of the wheel carriers. Prior to this operation the lower bump stops have to be removed.

LAMBRETTA 125-150 LI SERIES III

Number produced: 125 LI III		
Dec	1961	3,125
Jan/Dec	1962	48,351
Jan/Dec	1963	50,465
Jan/Dec	1964	25,347
Jan/Nov	1965	15,952
Jan/June	1966	2,022
Sept/Nov	1967	1,472
(frame prefix LI 4)		
Total		**146,734**

Number produced: 150 LI III	
Jan/Dec 1962	48,717
Jan/Dec 1963	48,021
Jan/Dec 1964	17,279
Jan/Dec 1965	17,006
Jan/Dec 1966	10,931
Jan/May 1967	1,028
TotalL	**142,982**

Frame numbering sequence from 125 LI III:
1.001
From 07/63 95.001
From 09/67 148.000
(prefix LI 4)

Frame numbering sequence from 150 LI III:
600.001

Identification details 125-150 LI

Version I 1962
LI II-type footboard tunnel (width between the two descending sides: 120 mm), side-panel anti-vibration buffers without springs, speedometer cable with small, square dial (LI 2-type). Electrical system with battery (150 only) and single wire to the off switch (125 only).

Version II end 1962 to mid-1965
Larger footboard tunnel (width between the two descending sides: 132 mm), speedometer cable with large dial, electrical system without battery and with the two cylinders unified, side-panel anti-vibration buffers fitted with small metal springs (from mid-1964).

Version III from mid-1965 to May 1967
Chromed ring between handlebar and leg-shield eliminated, side-panel clamps simplified, now without cog (from Jan. 1966).

Version IV September-November 1967 (125 only)
Frame with LI 4 prefix, side-panels with no aluminium handles, rectangular front badge, "Lambretta Innocenti" rear script, different colour scheme (see table).

Colour schemes 150 LI

Body colour parts
Fork, frame, leg-shield, fuel tank, rear floorboards, handlebar and headset, front mudguard, rear mudguard, floorboard tunnel, wheel hubs, front brake shoe backing plate, wheel rims, saddle frames and large central springs, spare wheel holder, cylinder head air intake manifold (2 pieces), glovebox and lid, tail-light body, fuel tap hatch, stand, stand mudguard, , right-hand rear floorboard L-bracket, battery holder strap, air box, filter carrier and air intake beneath saddle fuel tank support strap (from 1963). The headlamp cowling, the horn grille and the side-panels are painted in the following colour variants: New Blue, Nile Green, Ruby Red.

Colour schemes 125 LI

Body colour parts
Fork, frame, leg-shield, side-panels, rear floorboards, headlamp cowl and horn grille, handlebar and headset, handlebar lever carriers, fuel tank, front mudguard, rear mudguard, floorboard tunnel, wheel hubs, front brake shoe backing plate, wheel rims, saddle frames and large central springs, spare wheel holder, cylinder head air intake manifold (2 pieces), glovebox and lid, tail-light body, fuel tap hatch, stand, stand mudguard, right-hand rear floorboard L-bracket, air box, filter carrier and air intake beneath saddle fuel tank support strap (from 1963).

Version IV LI 4 only
The glovebox, fuel tank, cylinder head air intake manifold (2 pieces), headlamp cowling, front mudguard, rear mudguard, the air box and filter carrier and fuel tank support straps are painted in New White.

Finishes 125-150 LI

Black finish
Rear damper

Crankcase
Bare aluminium.

Carburettor
Carburettor body and float chamber cover bare aluminium, zinc-plated screws and fittings.

Control cable sheaths
Grey.

Saddles
Black imitation leather with "Innocenti" rear script.

Silencer
Aluminium.

Chromed parts

Frame
Brake pedal, frame tube cable circlip, "Lambretta LI" script on leg-shield, ring beneath steeringhead, threaded kick-start lever bush.

Electrical parts
Headlamp bezel, right-hand light switch screws and cover.

Engine
Kick-start lever.

Zinc-plated parts

Front fork
Screws and pins, lower steeringhead bearing dust cap, wheel carriers.

Frame
All screws and bolts, special washers, bushes. Side-panel internal catches, side-panel locking plates.

Electrical parts
Rectifier box (150 LI).

Engine
Levers, studs, screws and nuts, oil caps, lubricators.

Wheels
Plain and cap nuts, bushes, wheel hub brake levers.

Burnished parts

Engine
Air filter pipe fixing spring (version III only).

Frame
Plates and shaped bar for side-panel catches, stand spring, brake pedal spring, fuel tank support straps (1962 only).

Polished parts

Frame
Fuel tap and choke levers, side-panel levers, handlebar levers, Lambretta script on side-panels, floorboard runners and ferrules, leg shield profile terminals, edges of rear badge mount, glovebox lock lever.

150 LI only
Handlebar lever carriers.

Electrical parts
Handlebar Off switch, light switch cover.

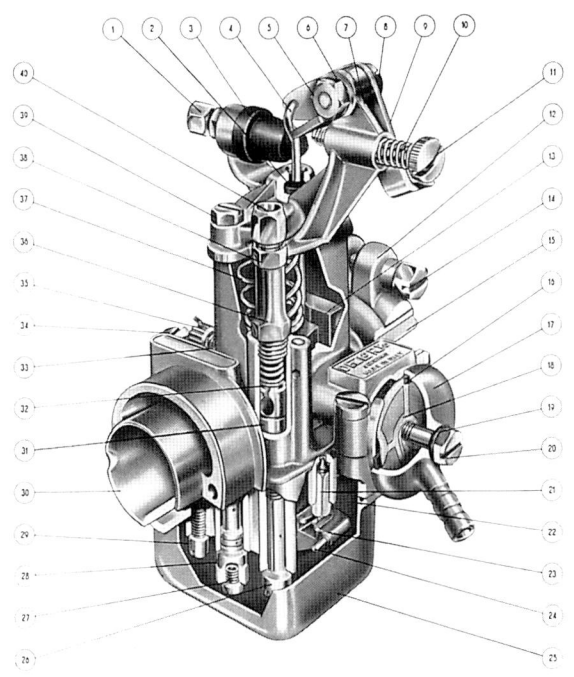

Lechler system colours

125 LI
Grey	8068
Iseo Blue	8035
Beige	Not available
Aquamarine blue	8030 (from 1964)
New White	8059 (internal parts LI 4 only)

150 LI
Grey	8068 (earliest examples only)
New White	8059

For the side-panels, the headlamp cowling and the horn grille:
New Blue	8038
Nile Green	8015
Ruby Red	8047

Maintenance data

Fuel/oil mixture:	2%
Spark plug:	Bosch 225/240 long thread
Engine oil:	SAE 90, 600 cc
Carburettor (125 LI):	Dell'Orto SH 1/18 max jet 98, min 42 Valve 1
Carburettor (150 LI):	Dell'Orto SH 1/18 max jet 105, min 45 Valve 1
Ignition advance:	22º - 24º 32-33 mm on flywheel circumference

CARBURETTOR SCHEME

1. Throttle valve cable tensioner screw
2. Lever gasket
3. Cable protection cap
4. Throttle valve linkage
5. Locking nut
6. Flexible washer
7. Throttle valve cover
8. Throttle lever pivot
9. Throttle valve linkage lever
10. Lever adjustment screw spring
11. Throttle valve lever qadjustment screw
12. Sleeve locking ring
13. Throttle valve
14. Sleeve ring locking screws
15. Insulating reduction
16. Inlet pipe gasket
17. Fuel pipe inlet duct
18. Fuel filter
19. Inlet pipe screw washer
20. Inlet pipe screw
21. Float needle
22. Float chamber
23. Carburettor float
24. Float pivot
25. Float chamber
26. Choke jet
27. Main Jet
28. Atomizer
29. Idle jet
30. Carburettor body
31. Choke valve
32. Choke valve return spring
33. Tick over screw spring
34. Float chamber fixing screws
35. Tick over adjustment screw
36. Choke valve cap
37. Throttle valve return spring
38. Cable tensioner locking nut
39. Fixing screws

LAMBRETTA 175 TV SERIES III - 200 TV

Number produced: 175TV III

Mar/Dec	1962	13,949
Jan/Dec	1963	14,554
Jan/Dec	1964	7,585
Jan/Oct	1965	1,706
Total		**37.749**

Number produced: 200 TV

Apr/Dec	1963	3,002
Feb/Dec	1964	6,092
Jan/Oct	1965	5,888
Total		**14,982**

Frame numbering sequence from 175 TV III: 500.001

Frame numbering sequence from 200 TV: follows progressive numbering of the 175 TV

Identification details

First version 1962-1963
Disc brake without white plastic grilles (earliest examples only). Smooth side-panels with no trim (LI-type), side-panel anti-vibration buffers all in rubber, rear "Lambretta 175 TV" script on white ground. Speedometer cable with small dial (until 12/62 then fitted with large dial). Four-pole flywheel magneto (6-pole from 09/62).

Second version December 1963 to end of production
Side-panels with aluminium trim (Special-type), side-panel anti-vibration buffers fitted with small metal springs, rear "Lambretta 175 TV" script on blue ground.

Colour schemes and finishes

First version:
Body parts in New White: fork, frame, rear floorboards, legshield, fuel tank, handlebar and headset, rear mudguard, floorboard tunnel, wheel hubs, front brake disc backing plate, wheel rims, spare wheel holder, cylinder head air intake manifold (2 pieces), glovebox and lid, tail-light body, fuel tap hatch, stand, stand mudguard, right-hand rear running-board L-bracket, battery holder strap, air box, filter carrier and air intake beneath the saddle, side-panels, front cowling, horn grille, front mudguard, fuel tank support strap (from 1963).

In the two-tone version the side-panels, the front cowling, the horn grille and the front mudguard may be: Coral Red (earliest examples only), Ruby Red, Light Yellow or Dark Grey.

ATTENTION, in the case of the version I first batch only: half of the cylinder cap (the spark plug side), the lower side of the central platform, the internal sides of the side panels and the rear mudguard are finished with a sound-deadening black paint NOT the body colour.

Second version:
Body parts in Metallic Blue: rear floorboards, fork, frame, legshield, handlebar and headset, floorboard tunnel, wheel hubs, front brake disc backing plate, wheel rims, spare wheel holder, glovebox lid, tail-light body, fuel tap hatch, stand, stand mudguard, right-hand rear running-board L-bracket air intake beneath the saddle, side-panels, front cowling, horn grille, front mudguard.
Parts in New White: fuel tank, rear mudguard, cylinder head air intake manifold (2 pieces), glovebox, air box, filter carrier, fuel tank support strap, battery support strap.

Black finish
Rear damper, saddle frame and clamp.

Fiat 690 metallic grey
Front dampers.

Crankcase
Bare aluminium.

Carburettor
Carburettor body and float chamber cover bare aluminium, zinc-plated, screws and fittings.

Control cable sheaths
Grey.

Saddles
Dark blue imitation leather with "Innocenti" or "Giuliari" rear script.

Silencer
Aluminium silver.

Chromed parts

Frame
Brake pedal, frame tube cable circlip, "Lambretta 175 TV" scripts, ring below handlebars, threaded kick-start lever bush.

Electrical parts
Headlamp bezel, right-hand light switch screws, ignition lock bezel.

Engine
Kick-start lever.

Wheels
Front wheel carriers (rough chromed without polishing).

Zinc-plated parts

Front fork
Screws and pins, lower steeringhead bearing dust cap.

FRONT DISC BRAKE

This innovation offers innumerable advantages, above all when you take into consideration the fact that the Lambretta 175/TV is a particularly rapid machine. The disc brake in fact confers greater confidence at high speeds, while avoiding problems with locking up at lower speeds and offering constant, progressive braking. Furthermore, the complete replacement of the brake pads is an extremely simple and very economical operation. Figure 2 shows a diagram of the disc brake composed of a central disc A that rotates with the wheel hub and two pads B and C that grip the disc during braking. Pad B is floating and controlled by the external lever. Pad C is fixed to the backing plate. During braking, pad B presses against the plate. This last is set laterally and is in turn pressed against the fixed pad C. The thickness of the ferodo friction material on pads is around 5 mm. The pads should be replaced when this thickness is reduced to around 2 mm. In order to adjust the disc brake, the screw located in correspondence with the brake lever is turned. When this adjustment has been made a number of times and the brake lever has been rotated excessively with respect to its normal position the following procedure should be adopted: completely detach the brake cable from the lever on the backing plates as shown in figure 3; use a box wrench to loosen the nut (see fig. 4) on the side of the fixed pad and, acting on screw inside the nut with a 4 mm wrench for internal thread, fully tighten the said screw.

Having tightened the screw, turn it back one revolution and lock it again with the nut. At this point the fixed pad is locked once more.

Reattach the brake cable to its lever and set the tension via the thread nipple. Braking should begin as soon as the handlebar lever is pulled.

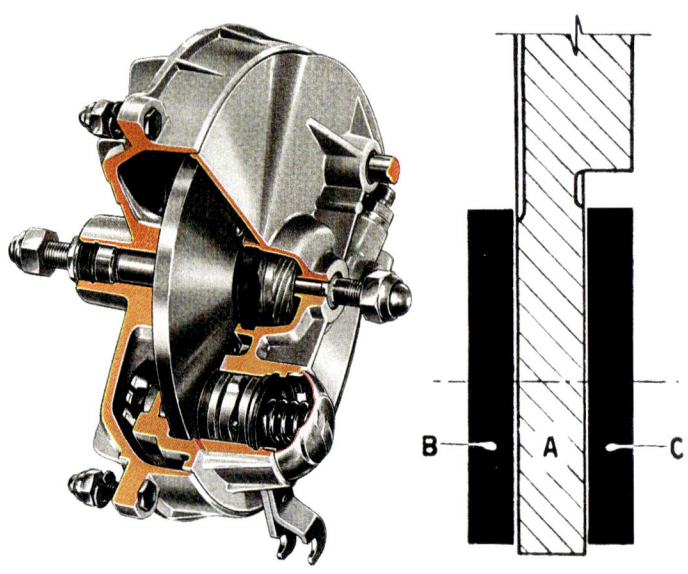

Frame

All screws and bolts, special washers, bushes, internal side-panel clasps.

Electrical parts

Rectifier box cover.

Engine

Levers, studs, nuts and bolts, lubricators, oil caps.

Wheels

Plain and cap nuts, bushes, wheel hub brake levers, disc brake lever cover.

Burnished parts

Engine

Air filter pipe fixing spring.

Frame

Stand spring, brake pedal spring, plates and shaped bars for side-panel catches, fuel tank support strap (Version I only 1962).

Polished parts

Frame

Fuel tap and choke levers, side-panel levers, floorboard runners and ferrules, leg shield profile terminals, handlebar lever carriers, rear badge mount frame, levers, trim and "Lambretta" scripts on side-panels, glovebox lock lever.

Electrical parts

Handlebar light switch cover.

Lechler system colours

175 TV III - 200 TV first version
Single colour model:
New White　　　　　　　8059
Two-tone model:
New White　　　　　　　8059 for the bodywork
For the side-panels, front cowling, horn grille and front mudguard:
Dark Grey　　　　　　　8071
Coral Red　　　　　　　8065 (earliest examples only)
Ruby Red　　　　　　　8047
Light Yellow　　　　　　8064

175 TV III - 200 TV second version:
Metallic Blue　　　　　　8062 (for the bodywork)
New White　　　　　　　8059 (for the internal parts)

Maintenance data

Fuel/oil mixture:　　　　4%
Spark plug:　　　　　　Bosch 225/240 long thread
Engine oil:　　　　　　 SAE 90, 600 cc
Carburettor (175):　　　Dell'Orto SH 1/20
　　　　　　　　　　　 max jet 106, min 50 Valve 1
Carburettor (200):　　　Dell'Orto SH 1/20
　　　　　　　　　　　 max jet 108, min 48 Valve 1
Ignition advance:　　　　22º - 24º 32-33 mm
　　　　　　　　　　　 on flywheel circumference

LAMBRETTA 50-100- 125 3m - 125 4m JUNIOR

Number produced: 50 J		
Oct/Dec	1964	2,798
Jan/Dec	1965	9,639
Jan/Aug	1966	9,639

50 J new 125 4m-type frame

Sep/Dec	1966	16,080
Jan/Dec	1967	30,902
Jan	1968	1,985
Total		69.988

Number produced: 100 J		
Mar/Dec	1964	14,084
Feb/Nov	1965	3,558
Total		17,642

Number produced: 125 J 3m

Sep/Dec	1964	6,483
Jan/Dec	1965	10,379
Feb/Sept	1966	4,789
Total		21,651

Number produced: 125 J 4m

May/Nov	1966	8,810
Jan/Nov	1967	2,730
Jan/Dec	1968	4,511
April	1969	1
Total		16,052

Frame numbering sequence from 50 J: 400.001

Frame numbering sequence from 100 J: 800.001

Frame numbering sequence from 125 J 3m: 600.001

Frame numbering sequence from 125 J 4m: 150.001

Identification details 50 J

First version 1964
9-inch wheels, wide leg-shield with no rubber edge trim, aluminium kick-start pedal, part below tail-light smooth, front fork with screw fitting for the dampers.

Second version 1965 - mid-1966
9-inch wheels, wide leg-shield with rubber edge trim, chromed metal kick-start lever, front fork with press-in dampers. Part below the tail-light stamped and carrying J50 script (from March 1966). Simplified side-panel clasps without cog (from January 1966).

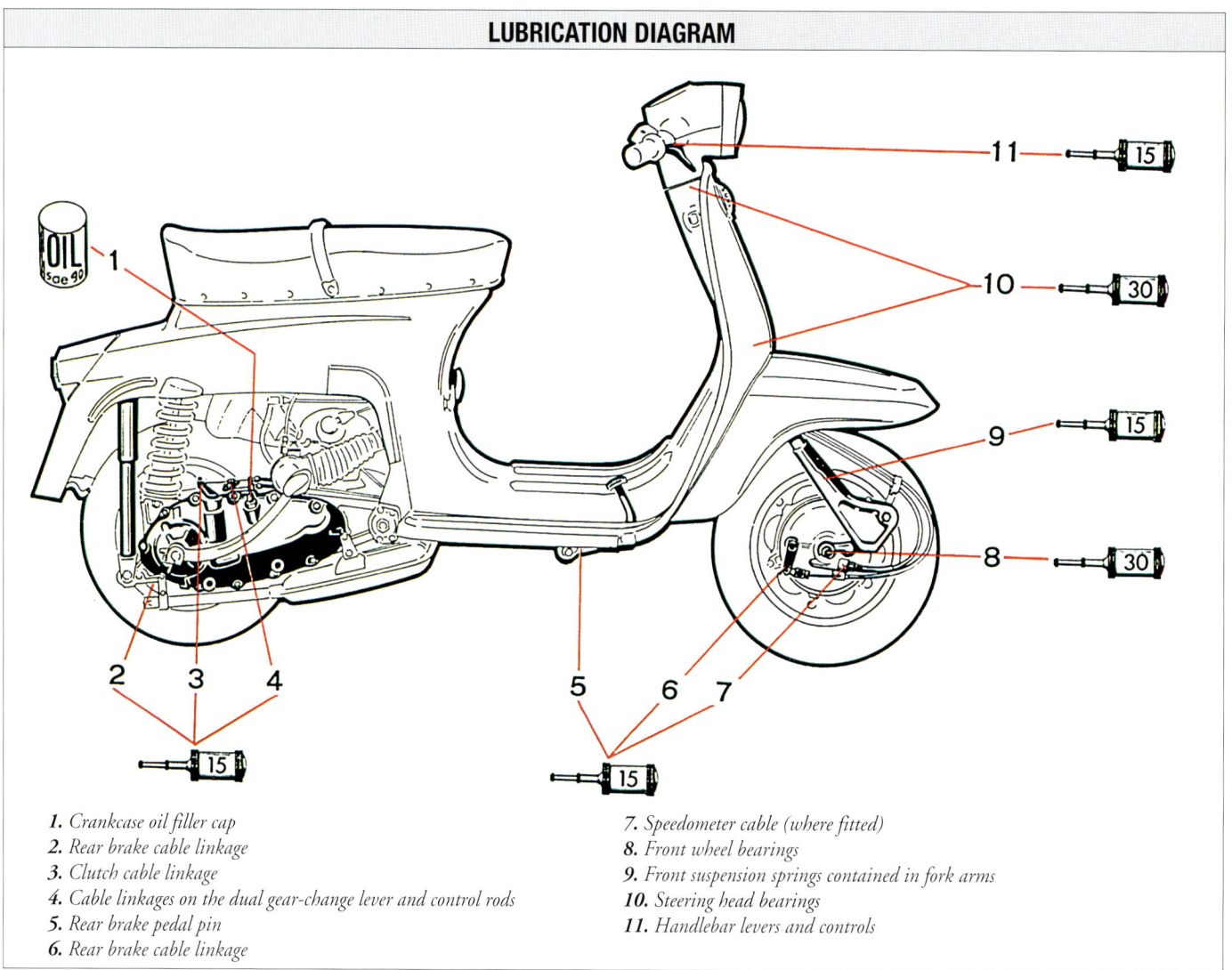

LUBRICATION DIAGRAM

1. Crankcase oil filler cap
2. Rear brake cable linkage
3. Clutch cable linkage
4. Cable linkages on the dual gear-change lever and control rods
5. Rear brake pedal pin
6. Rear brake cable linkage
7. Speedometer cable (where fitted)
8. Front wheel bearings
9. Front suspension springs contained in fork arms
10. Steering head bearings
11. Handlebar levers and controls

Third version mid-1966 - 1967 (official denomination "Model '66")
New 125 4m-type frame with narrower leg-shield, 9-inch wheels, longer saddle frame, part below the tail-light stamped and carrying J50 script, engine Silent Blocs reinforced.

Third version, last batch late-1967 - early-1968
Side-panels with DL-type concealed clasps.

Identification details 100 J

No modifications of note during the course of production except for the adoption of a rectangular rather than round steering lock from December 1964.

Identification details 125 J3m

Version I through to December 1964
Cylindrical steering lock housing, front fork with screw fitting for the dampers.

Version II 1965-1966
Rectangular steering lock housing, front fork with press-in dampers. Simplified side-panel clasps without cog (from January 1966).

ATTENTION: it is possible to find some examples of the 125 3m with the 1w25 4m frame. These are Lambrettas that have had their frame replaced under guarantee with one from the later versions. They cannot, therefore be considered as a final production batch.

Identification details: 125 4m

No modifications of note during the course of production. A version was prepared for export markets with a pivoting front mudguard and a false front cowling.

Colour schemes model 50
(through to mid-1967) - 100 - 125 3 and 4m:

Body colour parts
Fork, frame, front mudguard, side-panels, handlebar and headset, wheel hubs, front brake shoe backing plate, wheel rims, spare wheel holder, cylinder head air intake manifold (2 pieces), tail-light body, stand, rear license plate holder (50).

Colour schemes 50 J late-1967 - Jan. 1968

Body colour parts
Fork, frame, front mudguard, side-panels, handlebar and headset, tail-light body, stand, rear license plate holder.

Carter aluminium 8081
Wheel hubs, front brake shoe backing plate, wheel rims, spare wheel holder.

New White
Cylinder head air intake manifold (2 pieces).

Finishes

Grey primer
Fuel tank, air intake manifold (2 pieces) J100 first version ONLY.

Black finish
Saddle frame.

Aluminium
Rear damper.

Crankcase
Bare aluminium.

Carburettor
Carburettor body and float chamber cover bare aluminium, zinc-plated screws and fittings.

Control cable sheaths
Grey.

Saddles
Black imitation leather 50 J version I and II, 100 J and 125 J 3m. Dark blue imitation leather J 50 version III (mod. '66) and 125 4m. All with "Innocenti" rear script.

Silencer
Painted aluminium silver.

Chromed parts

Frame
Brake pedal, all leg-shield scripts, threaded kick-start lever bush, rear J 50 script.

Electrical parts
Headlamp bezel, light switch cover, horn grille.

Engine
Kick-start lever (if in steel).

Zinc-plated parts

Front fork
Screws and pins, wheel carriers.

Frame
All screws and bolts, special washers, bushes, stand mounting plates

Engine
Levers, studs, nuts and bolts, oil caps.

Wheels
Plain and cap nuts, bushes, wheel hub brake levers.

Burnished parts

Engine
Air filter pipe fixing spring.

Frame
Plates and shaped bars for side-panel catches, stand spring, brake pedal spring, large rear suspension spring.

Polished parts

Frame
Fuel tap and choke levers, side-panel levers, handlebar levers, handlebar lever carriers, leg-shield profile terminals.

Lechler system colours

50J versions I and II
New White	8059
Ruby Red	8047
Two-tone model:	
Light olive green	8079 (for the bodywork)
Dark olive green	8078 (for the side-panels)
New White	8059 (for the bodywork)
New Blue	8038 (for the side-panels)
Ruby Red	8047 (for the side-panels)

50J version III:
New White	8059
Aquamarine Blue	8030
Purple	8069
Apple Green	8039

100J:
Light Ivory	8054

125 J3m:
Metallic Grey	8060
Metallic Blue	8062

125 J4m
Blue	04T Pastel Blue A (Suzuki)

Maintenance data

Fuel/oil mixture:	2%
Spark plug:	Bosch 225/240 long thread
Engine oil:	SAE 90, 360 g.
Carburettor (50):	Dell'Orto SH 18/12 max jet 62, min 40 - Valve 1
Carburettor (100-125):	Dell'Orto SH 18/16 max jet 70, min 40 - Valve 1
Carburettor (125 4m):	Dell'Orto SH 18/16 max jet 72, min 40 - Valve 1
Ignition advance (50):	20° - 22° 1.6-2 mm ahead of Top Dead Centre
Ignition advance (100-125):	23° - 25° 2.4-2.8 mm ahead of Top Dead Centre

CYLINDER AND PISTON ASSEMBLY TOLERANCES AND WEAR LIMITS

TIPO	Selezione	MONTAGGIO NORMALE					1ª MAGGIORAZIONE					2ª MAGGIORAZIONE					3ª MAGGIORAZIONE					Gioco al Montagg. b - a	Gioco al limite di usura b - a
		CILINDRO		PISTONE		Seg-men.	CILINDRO		PISTONE		Seg-men.	CILINDRO		PISTONE		Seg-men.	CILINDRO		PISTONE		Seg-men.		
		Part.	Diametro mm. b	Part.	Diametro mm. a	Part.	Part.	Diametro mm. b	Part.	Diametro mm. a	Part.	Part.	Diametro mm. b	Part.	Diametro mm. a	Part.	Part.	Diametro mm. b	Part.	Diametro mm. a	Part.		
j 50	−	20151060	38.0 0.000 0.006	20151020	37.0 0.961 0.967	20151008	20151030	38.2 0.000 0.006		37.2 0.961 0.967	20151017	20151040	38.4 0.000 0.006		37.4 0.961 0.967	20151018	20151050	38.6 0.000 0.006		37.6 0.961 0.967	20151019	Min. 0,033 mm	
	0		0.007 0.013		0.968 0.974			0.007 0.013		0.968 0.974			0.007 0.013		0.968 0.974			0.007 0.013		0.968 0.974			
	+		0.014 0.020		0.975 0.981			0.014 0.020		0.975 0.981			0.014 0.020		0.975 0.981			0.014 0.020		0.975 0.981			
Cento	−	20051060	51.0 0.000 0.006	20051020	50.0 0.961 0.967	20051008	20051030	51.2 0.000 0.006		50.2 0.961 0.967	20051017	20051040	51.4 0.000 0.006		50.4 0.961 0.967	20051018	20051050	51.6 0.000 0.006		50.6 0.961 0.967	20051019	Max 0,045 mm	0,15 mm
	0		0.007 0.013		0.968 0.974			0.007 0.013		0.968 0.974			0.007 0.013		0.968 0.974			0.007 0.013		0.968 0.974			
	+		0.014 0.020		0.975 0.981			0.014 0.020		0.975 0.981			0.014 0.020		0.975 0.981			0.014 0.020		0.975 0.981			
125m4 - j125	−	20251060	57.0 0.000 0.006	20351020-20251020	56.0 0.960 0.966	20251008	20351030-20251030	57.2 0.000 0.006		56.2 0.960 0.966	20251017	20351040-20251040	57.4 0.000 0.006		56.4 0.960 0.966	2C251018	20351050-20251050	57.6 0.000 0.006		56.6 0.960 0.966	20251019	Min. 0,034 mm	
	0		0.007 0.013		0.967 0.973			0.007 0.013		0.967 0.973			0.007 0.013		0.967 0.973			0.007 0.013		0.967 0.973			
	+		0.014 0.020		0.974 0.980			0.014 0.020		0.974 0.980			0.014 0.020		0.974 0.980			0.014 0.020		0.974 0.980		Max 0,046 mm	

LAMBRETTA 125 - 150 SPECIAL (GOLDEN - SILVER)

Number produced: 150 S

Sep/Dec	1963	7,951
Jan/Dec	1964	36,022
Jan/Dec	1965	16,005
Jan/Oct	1966	9,551
Total		**69,529**

Number produced: 125 S

Oct/Dec	1965	4,196
Jan/Dec	1966	13,178
Jan/Dec	1967	8,442
Jan/Dec	1968	4,010
Jan	1969	15
Total		**29,841**

Frame numbering sequence from 150 S:
200.001

Frame numbering sequence from 125 S:
850.001

Identification details 150 S

First version April 1965
Side-panel anti-vibration buffers all rubber (until mid-1964), buffers with metal spring (after mid-1964), single "Special" script on right side of leg-shield.

Second version May 1965 to September 1965
Additional "Golden" or "Silver" script (according to the bodywork colour) above the leg-shield "Special" script.

Third version October 1965 - to end of production
Chromed ring between handlebar and leg-shield eliminated, side-panel clasps without cog (from Jan. 1966).

Identification details 125 S

First version October 1965 - early 1968
Front shield badge, painted metal glovebox, side-panel clasps without cog (from Jan. '66).

Second version early 1968 - late 1968
Rectangular front badge in aluminium, glovebox in grey plastic.

Third version - very last examples
Side-panels without aluminium handles, different colour scheme, 8 mm bolts with 13 mm heads.

Colour schemes 125-150

Body colour parts
Fork, frame, leg-shield, rear floorboards, handlebar and headset, rear mudguard, floorboard tunnel, wheel hubs, front brake shoe backing plate, wheel rims, spare wheel holder, glovebox lid, tail-light body, fuel tap hatch, stand, stand mudguard, right-hand rear floorboard L-bracket, side-panels, front cowling, horn grille, front mudguard.

New White
Fuel tank, rear mudguard, cylinder head air intake manifold (2 pieces), air box, filter carrier and air intake beneath saddle, fuel tank support strap, glovebox (when in metal).

125 S - very last examples

White Thorn body parts
Frame, leg-shield, handlebar and headset, rear floorboards, floorboard tunnel, glovebox lid, tail-light body, right-hand rear floorboard L-bracket, air intake beneath saddle, side-panels front cowling, horn grille, front mudguard, rear mudguard, cylinder head air intake manifold (2 pieces), air box, filter carrier and air intake beneath saddle, fuel tank support strap, fork, stand, stand mudguard.

Carter aluminium 8081
Fork, wheel hubs, front brake shoe backing plate, wheel rims, spare wheel holder, stand, stand mudguard. The plastic glovebox remained grey.

Finishes 125-150

Black finish
Rear damper, saddle frame and catch.

Crankcase
Bare aluminium.

Carburettor
Carburettor body and float chamber cover bare aluminium, zinc-plated screws and fittings.

Control cable sheaths
Grey.

Saddles
150 S - Silver: black imitation leather with "Innocenti" or "Giuliari" rear script.
125 S: dark blue imitation leather with "Innocenti" or "Giuliari" rear script.
150 S Golden: green imitation leather with "Innocenti" or "Giuliari" script.

Silencer
Aluminium silver.

Chromed parts

Frame
Brake pedal, frame tube cable circlip, all leg-shield scripts, ring beneath steeringhead, threaded kick-start lever bush.

Electrical parts
Headlamp bezel, right-hand light switch screws and cover, ignition barrel bezel.

Engine
Kick-start lever.

Zinc-plated parts

Front fork
Screws and pins, lower steeringhead bearing dust cap, wheel carriers.

Frame
All screws and bolts, special washers, bushes. Side-panel internal catches.

Engine
Levers, studs, screws and nuts, oil caps, lubricators.

Wheels
Plain and cap nuts, bushes, wheel hub brake levers.

Burnished parts

Engine
Air filter pipe fixing spring.

Frame
Stand spring, brake pedal spring, plates and shaped bar for side-panel catches.

Polished parts

Frame
Fuel tap and choke levers, floorboard runners and ferrules, leg shield profile terminals, handlebar levers and lever carriers, rear badge mount side-panel levers, trim and "Lambretta" scripts, glovebox lock lever.

Electrical parts
Handlebar light switch cover.

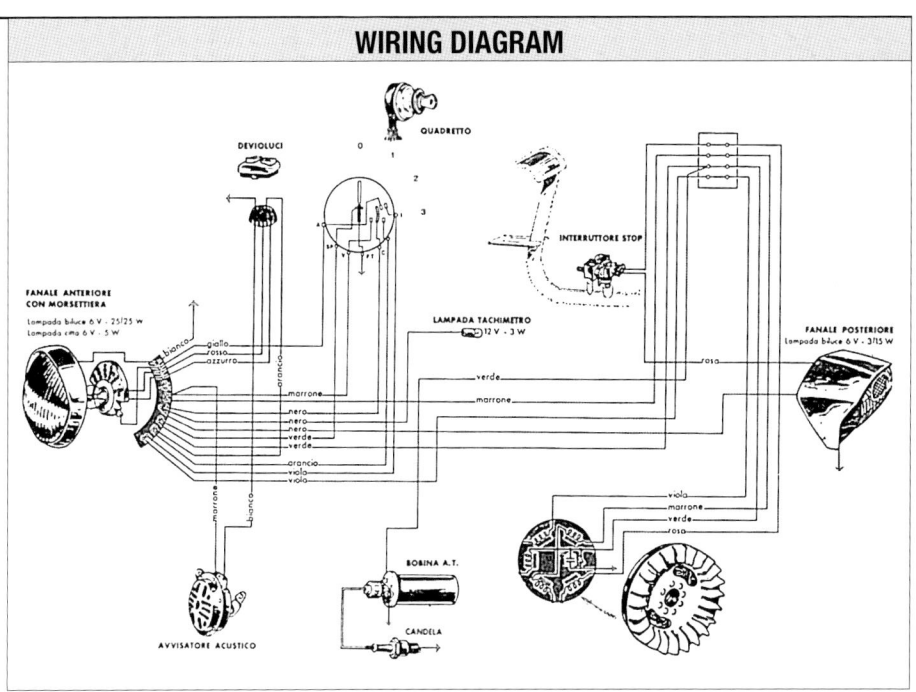

WIRING DIAGRAM

Lechler system colours

150 S

Metallic Grey	8060 "Silver"
Light Metallic Gold	8063 "Golden"
New White	8059 (internal bodywork parts only)

125 S

Metallic Blue	8061
White Thorn	8082 (last examples only)
New White	8059 (internal bodywork parts only)
Carter aluminium (wheels)	8081 (last examples only)

Maintenance data

Fuel/oil mixture:	2%
Spark plug:	Bosch 225/240 long thread
Engine oil:	SAE 90, 600 cc
Carburettor (150 S):	Dell'Orto SH 1/18 max jet 101, min 45 - Valve 1
Carburettor (125 S):	Dell'Orto SH 1/18 max jet 107, min 45 - Valve 1
Ignition advance:	22° - 24° 32-33 mm on flywheel circumference.

LAMBRETTA 150 SX - 200 SX

Number produced: 150 SX		
Oct/Dec	1966	3,570
Jan/Dec	1967	13,657
Jan/Dec	1968	13,844
Jan	1969	167
Total		31,238

Number produced: 200 SX		
Jan/Dec	1966	12,641
Jan/Dec	1967	4,632
Jan/Dec	1968	3,500
Jan 1968		4,010
Jan 1969		10
Total		20,783

Frame numbering sequence from 150 SX:
750.001

Frame numbering sequence from 125 S:
830.001

Identification details

First version through to early 1968
Shield front badge, glovebox in painted metal, front fork with bump-stops fixed with screws.

Second version early 1968 - autumn 1968
Rectangular front badge in aluminium, glovebox in grey plastic, front fork with press-in bump stops.

Final batch 1968
Side-panels without aluminium clasps (DL-type fixtures). Addition chrome trim on the front mudguard and polished horn grille on 200 SX model.

Last examples
8 mm bolts with 13 mm heads.

Colour schemes

200 SX
Bodywork in New White
Fork, frame, leg-shield, handlebar and headset, rear floorboards, floorboard tunnel, wheel hubs, front brake disc backing plate, wheel rims, spare wheel holder, glovebox lid (if in metal), tail-light body, fuel tap hatch, stand, stand mudguard, right-hand rear floorboard L-bracket, air intake beneath saddle, side-panels, front cowling, horn grille, front mudguard, battery support strap, fuel tank, cylinder head air intake manifold (2 pieces), glovebox, rear mudguard, air box, filter carrier and fuel tank support strap.

Fiat 690 metallic grey
Front dampers.

150 SX I-II:
Spring Grey or Apple Green body parts
Fork, frame, leg-shield, handlebar and headset, rear floorboards, floorboard tunnel, wheel hubs, front brake shoe backing plate, wheel rims, spare wheel holder, glovebox lid, tail-light body, fuel tap hatch, stand, stand mudguard, right-hand rear floorboard L-bracket, air intake beneath saddle, side-panels, front cowling, front mudguard.

On the Apple Green II batch version, wheels and wheel hubs were painted Aluminium 8081.

New White
Fuel tank, rear mudguard, cylinder head air intake manifold (2 pieces), glovebox (if in metal), air box, filter carrier, fuel tank support strap.

150 - 200 SX final batch
Bodywork in Thorn White
Frame, leg-shield, handlebar and headset, rear floorboards, floorboard tunnel, glovebox lid, tail-light body, fuel tap hatch, right-hand rear floorboard L-bracket, air intake beneath saddle, side-panels, front cowling, front mudguard, fuel tank, rear mudguard, air box, filter carrier and fuel tank support strap. stand, stand mudguard, cylinder head air intake manifold (2 pieces), horn grille, battery support strap, fuel tank, glovebox, rear mudguard, fork, stand, stand mudguard.

Aluminium carter 8081
Wheel rims, wheel hubs, front brake shoe backing plate, wheel rims, spare wheel holder.

Finishes

Black finish
Rear damper, saddle frame and catch.

Crankcase
Bare aluminium.

Carburettor
Carburettor body and float chamber cover bare aluminium, zinc-plated screws and fittings.

Control cable sheaths
Grey.

Saddles
150 SX black imitation leather with "Innocenti" or "Giuliari" rear script. 200 SX dark red imitation leather with "Innocenti" or "Giuliari" rear script.

Silencer
Aluminium silver.

Chromed parts

Frame
Brake pedal, frame tube cable circlip, all leg-shield scripts, threaded kick-start lever bush, front mudguard trim (150 SX and very last 200 SX examples).

Electrical parts
Headlamp bezel, right-hand light switch screws and cover, ignition barrel bezel.

Engine
Kick-start lever.

Zinc-plated parts

Front fork
Screws and pins, lower steeringhead bearing dust cap, wheel carriers.

Frame
All screws and bolts, special washers, bushes. Side-panel internal catches.

Engine
Levers, studs, screws and nuts, oil caps, lubricators.

Wheels
Plain and cap nuts, bushes, wheel hub brake levers, disc brake lever cover.

Burnished parts

Engine
Air filter pipe fixing spring.

Frame
Stand spring, brake pedal spring, plates and shaped bar for side-panel catches.

Polished parts

Frame
Fuel tap and choke levers, floorboard runners and ferrules, leg shield profile terminals, handlebar levers and lever carriers, rear badge mount, side-panel levers, trim and "Lambretta" scripts. Horn grille (150 SX and last 200 SX examples).

Electrical parts
Handlebar light switch cover.

Lechler system colours

150 SX
Spring Grey	8070
Apple Green	8039
New White	8059 (internal bodywork parts only)

150 SX - 200 SX (final batch)
White Thorn	8082
Carter aluminium (wheels)	8081

200 SX
New White	8059

Maintenance data

Fuel/oil mixture:	4% (200 SX) 2% (150 SX)
Spark plug:	Bosch 225/240 long thread
Engine oil:	SAE 90, 600 cc
Carburettor (150 SX):	Dell'Orto SH 1/20 max jet 107, min 45 - Valve 2
Carburettor (200 SX):	Dell'Orto SH 1/20 max jet 103, min 48 - Valve 1
Ignition advance:	22º - 24º 32-33 mm on flywheel circumference

SILENT BLOCK

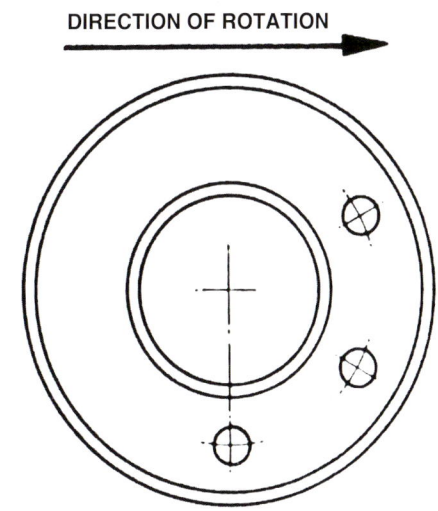

DIRECTION OF ROTATION

In order to reduce vibration transmitted by the engine to the frame, a new type of silent block has been fitted, as shown in figure 5 and 6. This new model will permit all vibration, particularly at high speeds, to be significantly reduced. The pivot whereby the engine is attached to the frame has been lengthened and the silent blocks are fitted ahead of the engine support lugs. Note that there are three holes in the rubber of the new silent blocks. These holes are designed to modify the elastic performance of the mount. The silent block must therefore be fitted the right way round. One hole should be pointing downwards while the other two should be facing the front of the vehicle. N.B. The silent blocks must not be cleaned with petrol or oil or dampened with oil as under the action of such liquids the rubber is subject to deterioration and loses its elasticity.

Bottom photo: detail of the arrangement of the control cables on the frame. This layout is applicable to the III version LI-TV - S - SX - DL.

LAMBRETTA 50 C-CL - 75 S-SL

Number produced: 50 C-CL
Mar/Dec 1968	20,665
Jan/Jun 1969	7,147
Total	**27,812**

Number produced: 75 S-SL
Aug/Dec 1968	4,542
Jan/Jun 1969	4,329
Feb/Dec 1970	531
Total	**9,402**

Frame numbering sequence from 50 C-CL:
575.001

Frame numbering sequence from 75 S-SL:
650.001

Identification details 50 C-CL 75 S-SL

First version through to early 1969
Lambretta script on left-hand side of the leg-shield above the 50 C or CL script, handlebar levers without ball-end, chromed grille behind the headlight without script.

Second version early 1969 to end of production
"Lambretta" script on leg-shield eliminated, rectangular LUI badge in the centre of the leg-shield, handlebar levers with ball-ends, chromed grille behind headlight with "Lambretta" script. In some cases, above the rectangular LUI badge, a small "Lambretta" script may be found.

Colour schemes and finishes

Body colour parts
Fork, frame, leg-shield, front and rear mudguard, frame tunnel inside leg-shield, fuel tank, headlight body (2-piece).

Aluminium crankcase finish 8081
Handlebar, wheel hubs, front brake shoe backing plate, wheel rims, stand, crankcase cover, brake pedal.

Gloss black
Saddle frame.

Matte black
Luggage rack, cylinder cover. 75 only: silencer grille (2-piece), license plate holder and tail-light.

Aluminium finish
Rear damper.

Crankcase
Bare aluminium. Crankcase cover painted aluminium 8081.

Carburettor
Carburettor body and float chamber cover bare aluminium, zinc-plated screws and fittings.

Control cable sheaths
Black.

Saddles
Black imitation leather. "Lambretta Innocenti" script.

Silencer
Aluminium (50), chromed (75).

Chromed parts

Frame
Front and rear scripts, rear damper spring.

Electrical parts
Headlamp bezel, light switch cover. Grille behind headlight with chromed and black ribs. Tail-light (50 CL).

Engine
Kick-start lever. Exhaust (75).

Zinc-plated parts

Front fork
Screws and pins, lower wheel carriers.

Frame
All screws and bolts, special washers, bushes. Stand fixing plates.

Horn button mounted on the Lui 50 C only. In black plastic with external electrical wiring.

Engine
Levers, studs, screws and nuts, oil caps, lubricators.

Wheels
Plain and cap nuts, bushes, wheel hub brake levers.

Burnished parts

Engine
Cast-iron exhaust header (75).

Frame
Stand spring, brake pedal spring.

Polished parts

Frame
Handlebar levers and lever carriers.

Lechler system colours

Crankcase aluminium	8081 (frame)	

50C
White Thorn	8082	

50 CL
Turquoise	8016	
Orange	8037	
Apple Green	8039	

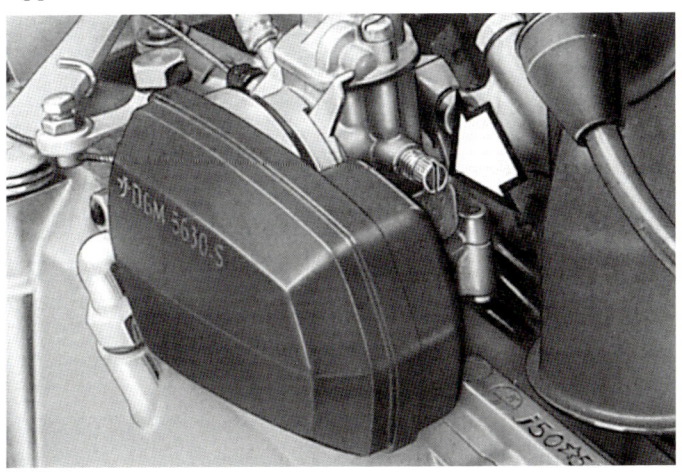

DIAGRAM OF THE LUBEMATIC SYSTEM

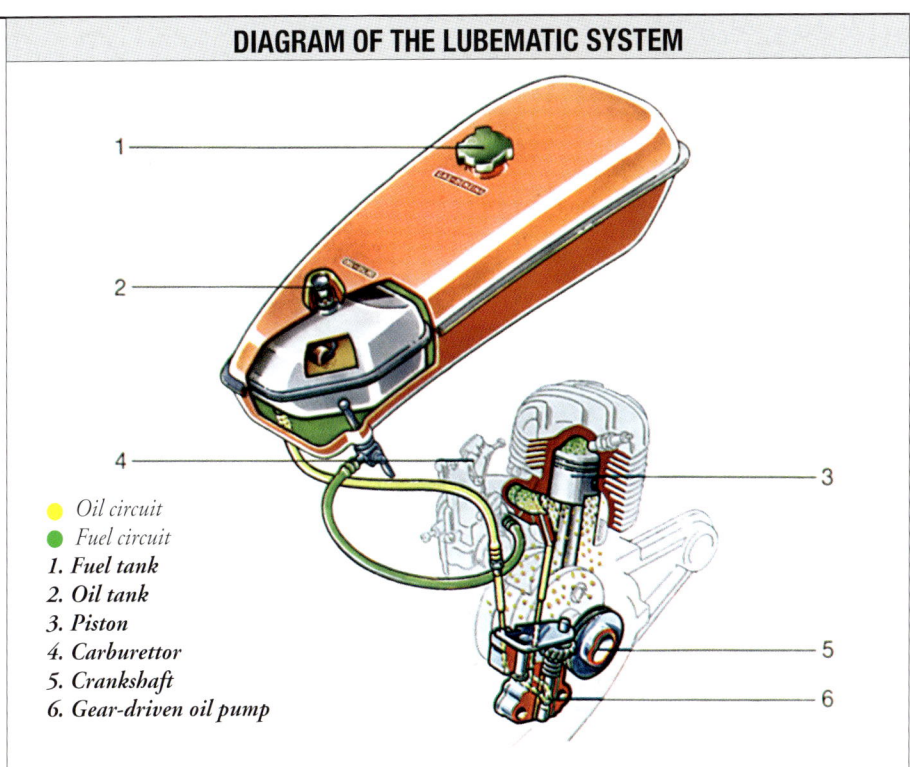

● *Oil circuit*
● *Fuel circuit*
1. *Fuel tank*
2. *Oil tank*
3. *Piston*
4. *Carburettor*
5. *Crankshaft*
6. *Gear-driven oil pump*

75 S-SL
Metallic Grey	8060
Ochre	8080

Maintenance data

Fuel/oil mixture:	2%
Spark plug:	Bosch 225/240 long thread
Engine oil:	SAE 90, 450 g (50) 620 g (75)
Carburettor (50):	Dell'Orto SH 14/12 max jet 52
Carburettor (75):	Dell'Orto SH 1/20 max jet 68, min 45 - Valve 1
Ignition advance	20° - 22° 1.65-2.01 mm ahead of Top Dead Centre

Left: the air filter box fitted to the 50 LUI. Square shaped and carrying the Innocenti emblem. The arrow indicates the idle adjustment screw.

LAMBRETTA 50 DE LUXE - SPECIAL

Number produced:
50 De Luxe
Jan/Dec	1968	15.097
Jan/Dec	1969	9,045
Jan/Oct	1970	4,710
Total		**28,852**

Number produced:
50 Special
Apr/Dec	1970	11,446
Jan/Apr	1970	2,153
Total		**13,599**

Frame numbering sequence from 50 e Luxe: 480.001

Frame numbering sequence from 50 Special: follows numbering and prefix of 50 DL

Identification details 50 DL

Lambretta script on left-hand side of the leg-shield above the 50 C or CL script, handlebar levers without ball-end, chromed grille behind the headlight without script.

Identification details 50 Special

Single-seat saddle, pressed-steel rear luggage rack, side-panel trim with 3 flames, footrest runners in aluminium with rubber inserts, 10"-wheels. No modifications of note during the course of production.

Colour schemes 50 De Luxe

Body colour parts
Fork, frame, front mudguard, side-panels, handlebar and headset, tail-light body, stand, luggage rack.

Carter aluminium 8081
Wheel hubs, front brake shoe backing plate, wheel rims, spare wheel holder, cylinder head air intake manifold (2 pieces).

COLOUR SCHEMES 50 Special

Body colour parts
Frame, front mudguard, side-panels, handlebar and headset, tail-light body.

Carter aluminium 8081
Fork, stand, wheel hubs, front brake shoe backing plate, wheel rims, spare wheel holder, cylinder head air intake manifold (2 pieces).

Finishes

Grey primer
Fuel tank.

Black
Saddle frame. Fuel tap and choke levers (50 S).

Aluminium finish
Rear damper.

Crankcase
Bare aluminium.

Carburettor
Carburettor body and float chamber cover bare aluminium, zinc-plated screws and fittings.

Control cable sheaths
Grey (50 DL), black (50 S).

Saddles
50 DL, dark blue imitation leather with rear "Lambretta Innocenti" script. 50 S, brown imitation leather in centre, black sides and descending rear section.

Silencer
Aluminium.

Chromed parts

Frame
Brake pedal, all leg-shield scripts, Special script on side-panel (in some cases a De Luxe script in chrome-plated brass may be found on the side-panels), lifting handle fixing plate and screws (50 S).

Engine oil caps:
1. filler
2. level
3. drain
Attention: on the standard production model, the black exhaust shown here would have been finished in aluminium silver.

Electrical parts
Headlamp bezel, light switch cover, horn grille.

Engine
Kick-start lever.

Zinc-plated parts

Front fork
Screws and pins, wheel carriers.

Frame
All screws and bolts, special washers, bushes. Stop plates for the shaped bars of the side-panel catches, stand fixing plates.

Engine
Levers, studs, screws and nuts, oil caps.

Wheels
Plain and cap nuts, bushes, wheel hub brake levers.

Burnished parts

Frame
Shaped bar for side-panel catch, stand spring, brake pedal spring, large rear suspension spring.

Polished parts

Frame
Handlebar levers and lever carriers, aluminium leg-shield border. 50 DL only: floorboard runners and ferrules, fuel tap and choke levers.

Lechler system colours

Carter aluminium (frame) 8081

50 De Luxe:
New White	8059
Aquamarine blue	8030
Apple Green	8039

50 Special:
Turquoise	8016
Red	8073
Ochre	8080

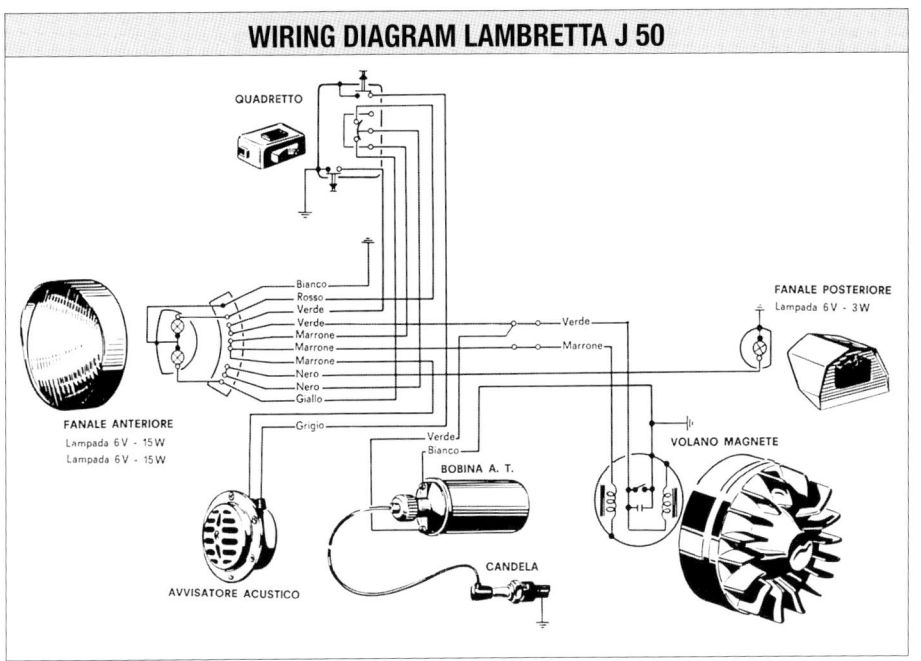

Maintenance data

Fuel/oil mixture:	2%
Spark plug:	Bosch 225/240 long thread
Engine oil:	SAE 90, 360 g
Carburettor:	Dell'Orto SH 18/12
	max jet 62, min 40, Valve 1
Ignition advance:	20° - 22° 1.6-2 mm
	ahead of Top Dead Centre.

LAMBRETTA 125 - 150 - 200 DL

Number produced: 125 DL		
Jan/Dec	1969	7,449
Jan/Dec	1970	6,441
Jan/Apr	1971	1,410
Total		15,300

Number produced: 150 DL		
Jan/Dec	1969	10,703
Jan/Dec	1970	8,204
Jan/Apr	1971	1,141
Total		20,048

Number produced: 200 DL		
Jan/Dec	1969	4,777
Jan/Dec	1970	3.824
Jan/Apr	1971	749
Total		9,350

Frame numbering sequence from 125 DL:
1.001

Frame numbering sequence from 150 DL:
200.001

Frame numbering sequence from 200 DL:
250.001

Identification details

First version to mid-1970
Cast-aluminium horn grille and dummy rear air intake, fuel tap hatch in painted metal.

Second version mid-1970 to end of production
Plastic horn grille, dummy rear air intake and fuel tap hatch.

Colour schemes and finishes

Body colour parts
Frame, leg-shield, handlebar and headset, rear floorboards, floorboard tunnel, glovebox lid, fuel tap hatch (if in metal), right-hand rear running-board L-bracket, air intake beneath the saddle, side-panels, front cowling, front mudguard, dummy air intake (if in metal).

White Thorn
Fuel tank, rear mudguard, cylinder head air intake manifold (2 pieces), air box, filter carrier, fuel tank support strap.

Carter aluminium 8081
Wheel rims, wheel hubs, front brake shoe backing plate, stand, stand mudguard, fork, spare wheel holder.
On the last examples of the 200 DL, the fork is painted in non-metallic light grey.
The plastic parts (glovebox, horn grille, fuel tap hatch, dummy rear air intake) are left unpainted black.

Black finish
Rear damper, horn grille, saddle frame and clamp, fuel tap, choke, glovebox handles.

Aluminium paint
Front dampers (200 DL only).

Crankcase
Bare aluminium.

Carburettor
Carburettor body and float chamber cover bare aluminium, zinc-plated, screws and fittings.

Control cable sheaths
Black.

Saddles
Black imitation leather with "Lambretta Innocenti" rear script.

Silencer
Aluminium silver.

Chromed parts

Frame
Brake pedal, frame tube cable circlip, "Lambretta" leg-shield script, oval badge on front cowling, rear "Innocenti" badge (black background).

Electrical parts
Headlamp bezel, ignition lock bezel.

Engine
Kick-start lever.

Zinc-plated parts

Front fork
Screws and pins, lower steeringhead bearing dust cap.

Frame
All screws and bolts, special washers, bushes, plates for the shaped bars of the side-panel catches.

Electrical parts
Handlebar light switch screws.

Engine
Levers, studs, nuts and bolts, lubricators, oil caps.

Wheels
Plain and cap nuts, bushes, wheel hub brake levers, disc brake lever cover (200).

Burnished parts

Engine
Air filter pipe fixing spring.

Frame
Stand spring, brake pedal spring, shaped bars for side-panel catches.

Polished parts

Frame
Handlebar levers and lever carriers.

Electrical parts
Handlebar light switch cover.

Lechler system colours

Carter aluminium (frame) 8081

125 DL
Thorn White	8082
Turquoise	8016

150 DL
Red	8073
Thorn White	8082

200 DL
Ochre	8080

Maintenance data

Fuel/oil mixture:	4% (200)
	2% (125-150)
Spark plug:	Bosch 225/240 long thread
Engine oil:	SAE 90, 600 cc
Carburettor (125):	Dell'Orto SH 1/20
	max jet 98, min 45 - Valve 2
Carburettor (150):	Dell'Orto SH 2/22
	max jet 118, min 45 - Valve 2
Carburettor (200):	Dell'Orto SH 2/22
	max jet 118, min 45 - Valve 1
Ignition advance:	22° - 24° 2.20-2.66 mm
	ahead of Top Dead Centre

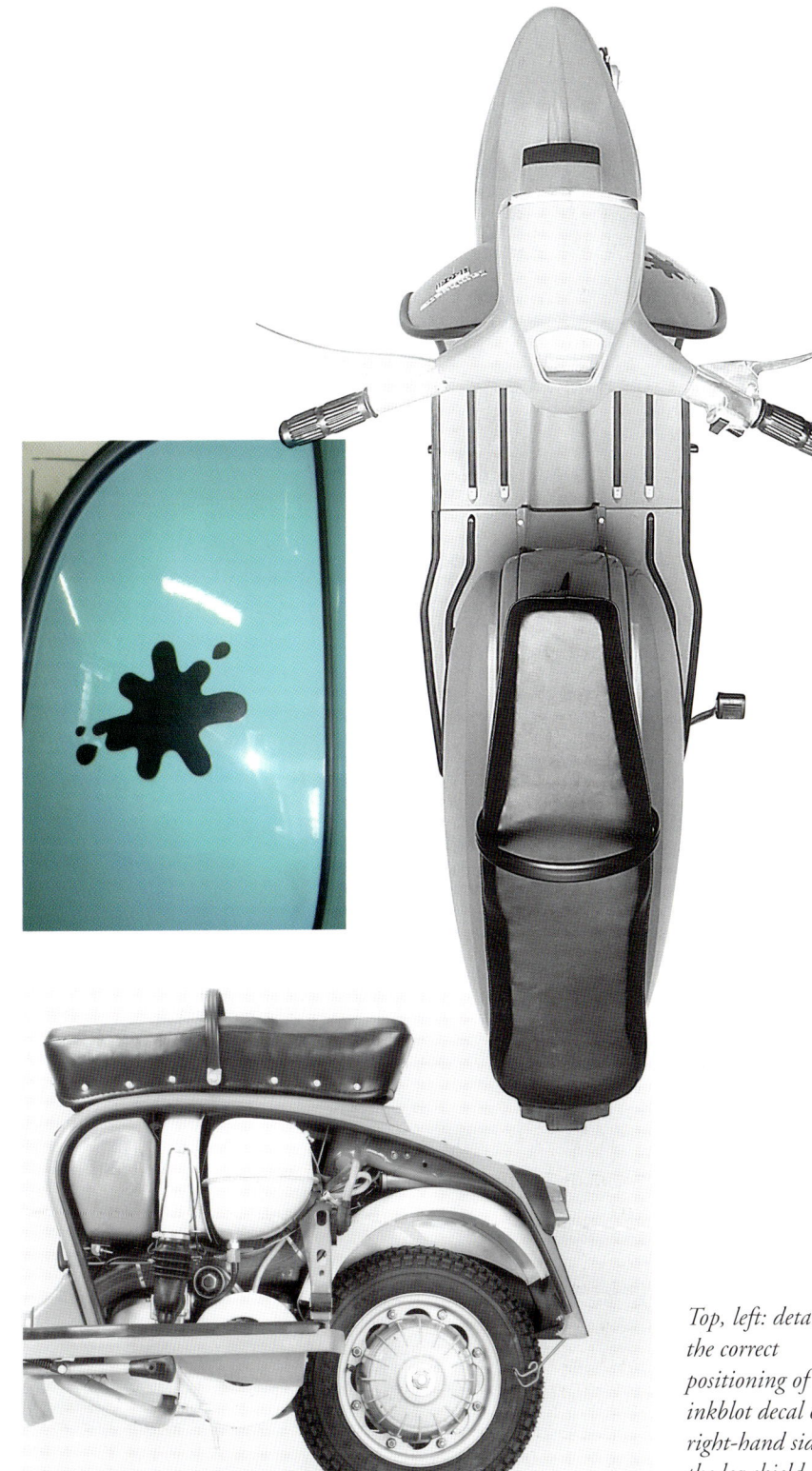

Top, left: detail of the correct positioning of the inkblot decal on the right-hand side of the leg-shield.

LAMBRETTA 48

Number produced: Type 57		
Aug/Dec	1955	5,928
Jan/Dec	1956	22,155
Jan/Dec	1957	6,826
May/Oct	1958	3,312

Number produced: Type 58		
Oct/Dec	1958	1,562
Jan/Dec	1959	10,504
Jan/Dec	1960	11,955
Jan/Mar	1961	981
Total		10,086

Frame numbering sequence from: 00.001

Identification details Type 57

First version to mid-1956
Stand in forged metal rod (from Feb. 1956 in pressed steel), flywheel side cover with chrome inset carrying "Lambretta" script (from the end of 1955 the script was directly cast into the cover), engine disengagement pivot and metal toolbox cover, rear hub with chain tensioner.

Second version to October 1958
Stand in pressed steel, engine disengagement pivot and toolbox cover in plastic, rear hub with no chain tensioner, external headlight bezel screws. Carburettor cap (from Sept. 1956), polished rear dampers (aluminium type, from Oct. 1956).

Identification details Type 58

First version to mid-1960
Twin-cable gear control, internal engine HT coil, cylinder head decompression device eliminated.

Second version to end of production
Handlebar lever carriers manufactured by outside firm with straight throttle actuation.

Colour schemes and finishes

Body colour parts
Fork, frame, front and rear mudguards, fuel tank, luggage rack, toolbox (only if in metal), headlamp, rear fork, rear dampers, stand (for model in pressed steel only).

Body parts in Fiat 690 Aluminium
Wheel hubs, front and rear brake shoe backing plates, saddle frame.

Crankcase
Painted Fiat 690 aluminium.

Carburettor
Carburettor body and tickler in bare aluminium, zinc-plated screws and fittings, semi-gloss carburettor cap.

Control cable sheaths
Grey.

Saddle
Black, medium grain imitation leather with "Innocenti" rear script.

Silencer
Body and circlip black, header chromed, bezel cadmium-plated.

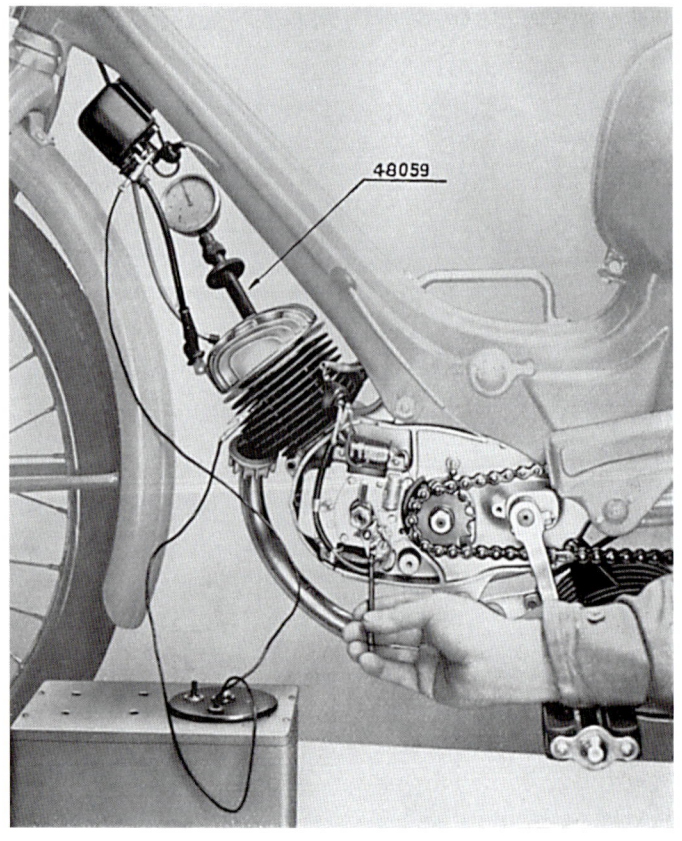

Right, instructions for the mounting of the ignition timing adjustment equipment.

Chromed parts

Frame
Handlebar, levers and details, rear dampers (reinforced type only).
Electrical parts
Headlamp and tail light bezels, horn grille, light switch cover.
Engine
Exhaust header and circlip, pedal cranks.
Wheels
Rims.

Cadmium-plated parts
(zinc-plated from 1959/1960)

Front fork
Front wheel carriers and nuts.
Frame
All screws and bolts, lubricators, steeringhead bearing caps, special washers, bushes, stand spring, saddle stem.
Electrical parts
Light switch circlip, air filter lever.
Engine
Levers, studs, screws.
Wheels
Nuts, bushes, wheel hub brake levers, rear cog, spokes.

Burnished parts

Frame
Crank pivots.
Engine
Bushes.

Polished parts

Frame
Lifting handle, handlebar lever carriers, dampers (aluminium reinforced type).

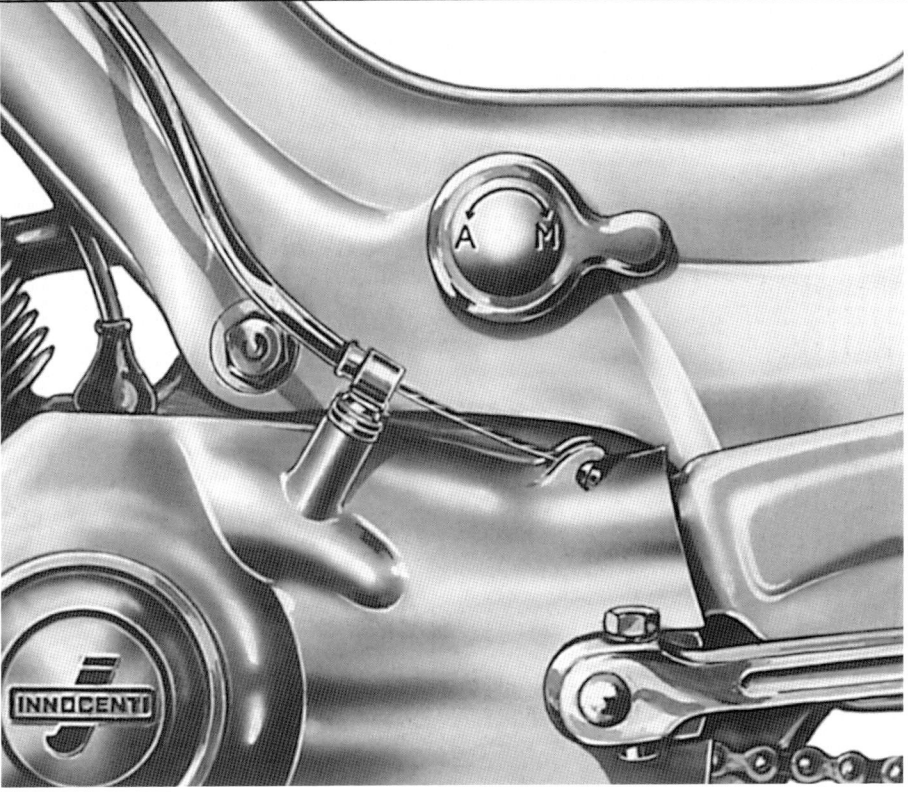

Lechler system colours

Earth Grey	8041
Pompei Red	8045
Lambro Grey	8034
Aluminium (engine and frame)	Fiat 690

Maintenance data

Fuel/oil mixture:	5%
Spark plug:	Bosch 225/240 long thread
Engine oil:	SAE 15/50, 400 g
Carburettor:	Dell'Orto T5-11S max jet 62 - Valve 50
Carburettor:	Dell'Orto T5-12S max jet 60 - Valve 50

The single wire gear change cable fitted to the first version of the Lambretta 48. In this case, note also the chromed round cover with the red script that characterised the earliest examples produced.

LAMBRETTA COLOUR GUIDE

This chapter illustrates the range of possible colour schemes found on Lambretta models built between 1947 and 1971.

During what proved to be a complex research process I drew exclusively on the official Innocenti documents: both those sent to the dealers and those destined for in-house use by the factory. Unfortunately, part of this documentation was destroyed after the dismantling of the Lambretta production line in 1972 and therefore in order to complete the work I had to rely on the memories and testimony of people who worked in the factory in the 1950s and '60s.

It has been a long and demanding process and is by no means finished: I am sure, in fact, that in time further documents will come to light that will complete the research and define even more precisely the Lambretta colour chart.

To this end, I would invite you all to let me know of any documentary material or Lambretta model with an unusual colour scheme so I can compile a form historic colour archve for each new edition.

We frequently find Lambrettas with the most diverse colour schemes and the most bizarre explanations for them: I would remind you that Innocenti was a large company with a complex and automated production cycle. It is clear, therefore, that it would have been difficult to satisfy requests for non-standard colour schemes. Normally, this kind of service was provided directly by the dealers who, in order to distinguish themselves from the competition, invented unique special colours or personalised styling modifications. In the case of examples modified in this way, the ASI or FMI identity certificate may still be requested as long as you can demonstrate with original photographs or receipts that the Lambretta in question actually left the dealer's in that form.

A number of models destined for the Swiss and German market were characterised by dual coachlines throughout the bodywork. I have yet to find documentation proving whether this unusual and extremely expensive finish was applied in the factory or by the local distributor. However, in this case too, should you want to apply for the ASI or FMI identity certificate it is absolutely vital that you present documentation proving that the scooter came from one of these countries.

Advice on colours:

For the oldest models (Tipo 125 D) the paint used on the wheel rims, the engine cover and other bodywork items (Fiat 690 aluminium) must be applied lightly, with no transparent coat, and should have a semi-gloss appearance.

You should always remember that the Lambretta was a very economical "people's" scooter; its paintwork was never that of a perfectly mirror-polished Rolls Royce, but rather the traditional paint finish of mass production vehicles.

In the case of metallic paint, it would be preferable to use the gloss type with no transparent coat.

Remember that on all Lambretta models the arrow and the numbers on the handlebar gear indicator were always painted in red.

On the LI-TV-S models the two screws fixing the right-hand passenger footboard support and the screws fixing the horn grille (when painted) were always painted in the same colour as the bodywork (as they were fitted prior to painting).

Again on the LI models, the single saddle and its central spring were always painted in the same colour as the bodywork, while the pin, the nut and the washer fixing the central spring were zinc-plated.

I have frequently seen perfectly restored Lambrettas with the rear hub left in unpainted aluminium: this is a serious error as the front and rear drums were always painted in aluminium grey or in the same colour as the bodywork, depending on the model.

A number of unusual colours are marked by a warning code; please read these carefully to avoid unnecessary work.

A - Specific colour used for a limited number of examples: in this case the ASI or FMI certification requires with no exception photographic documentation of the scooter prior to restoration proving that it was originally finished in that particular colour.

B - Colour offered towards the end of the model's production run: it is not possible to the use this colour for examples from prior production batches.

C - Colour only offered early in the production run: cannot be used on examples produced later.

D - Specific colour for models destined for export: in this case, in order to obtain ASI or FMI certification it is absolutely necessary that the Lambretta is accompanied by documentation proving that it was sold on an export market (registration documents or customs certificate).

E - This particular model, the LI 150 SX, is a 3rd series 150 LI with the frame and engine marked as a 150 SX; it may be recognised by the absence of engine cover clips (DL-type fixtures). Currently there is no information deriving from production data or historical details to help us better identify this model.

ALL THE LAMBRETTA COLOURS*

125A - Dark Olive Green 8022

125A - Dark Red 8020

125A - Light Blue 8017

125A - Ivory (colour not available)

125 B - Metallic Blue 8024

125 B - Metallic Red 8023

125 B - Metallic Green 8025

125 B - Metallic Bronze 8053

125 C - Light Olive Khaki 8027

125 C - Chamois 8011

125 C - Blue (colour not available) (A) (C)

125 LC - Light Olive Khaki 8027

125 LC - Chamois 8011

* The Lambretta colours shown on these pages are purely indicative; the Lechler codes indicated in this list are instead indispensable when referring to Lambretta paintwork.

125 LC - Light Blue (colour not available) (A) (C)

125 D - Olive Green 8021

125 D - Light Chamois 8055

125 D - Sand Beige 8029

125 LD - Olive Green 8021

125 LD - Light Chamois 8055

125 LD - Sand Beige 8029

125 LD '53 - Sand Beige 8029

125 E - Olive Green 8021

125 F - Sand Beige 8029

125 F - Light Grey 8012 (B)

150 D - Sand Beige 8029

150 D - Light Grey 8012 (B)

65

150 LD - Sand Beige 8029

150 LD - Light Grey 8012

150 LD - Light Grey 8012 with side-panels Emerald Green 8051 (D)

150 LD - Light Grey 8012 with side-panels Pompei Red 8045 (D)

150 LD - Light Grey 8012 with side-panels England Blue 8032 (D)

150 LD - Light Grey 8012 with side-panels Teal (colour not available) (D)

150 LD - Dark Red (D)

150 LD - Sky Light Blue 8043 (D)

150 LD elec. - Sand Beige 8029

150 LD elec. - Light Grey 8012 with side-panels, front cowling and front mudguard England Blue 8031

125 LD der. '56 - Sand Beige 8029

125 LD '57 - Earth Grey 8041

150 LD '57 - Earth Grey 8041 with side-panels, front cowling and handlebar fairing Tyrrhenian Blue Brazil C 401

150 LD '57 - Earth Grey 8041 with side-panels, front cowling and handlebar fairing Teal (colour not available) (D)

150 LD '57 - Earth Grey 8041 with side-panels, front cowling and handlebar fairing England Blue 8032 (D) | 150 LD '57 - Earth Grey 8041 with side-panels, front cowling and handlebar fairing Emerald Green 8051 (D) | 150 LD '57 - Earth Grey 8041 with side-panels, front cowling and handlebar fairing Antilles Brown 8044 (D)

150 LD '57 - Earth Grey 8041 with side-panels, front cowling and handlebar fairing Red 8012 (D) | 175 TV 1s. - Ivory 8028 | 175 TV 1s. - Ivory 8028 with side-panels, front cowling and handlebar fairing Antilles Brown 8044 (D)

125 LI 1s. - Dawn Grey 8019 | 125 LI 1s. - Dawn Grey 8019 with side-panels Dark Steel Grey 8040 | 150 LI 1s. - River Grey 8014

150 LI 1s. - Dawn Grey 8019 con with side-panels, front cowling and handlebar Flaminia Blue 8032 | 150 LI 1s. - Dawn Grey 8019 with side-panels, front cowling and handlebar Ruby Red 8047 | 150 LI 1s. - Dawn Grey 8019 with side-panels, front cowling and handlebar Nile Green 8015

150 LI 1s. - Dawn Grey 8019 with side-panels, front cowling and handlebar England Blue 8031

150 LI 1s. - Dawn Grey 8019 with side-panels, front cowling and handlebar Coral Red 8046

175 TV 2s. - Tyrrhenian Blue 8042

175 TV 2s. - Oriental Yellow 8049

175 TV 2s. - Opal Green (colour not available) (D)

175 TV 2s. - Sand (colour not available) (D)

125 LI 2s. - Dawn Grey 8019 with side-panels Dark Steel Grey 8040 (1959-1960)

125 LI 2s. - Whitethorn 8082 with side-panels Dark Steel Grey 8040 (1960-1961)

125 LI 2s. - Whitethorn 8082 with side-panels Orange Yellow (colour not available) (1960-1961) (D)

125 LI 2s. - Opal Green (colour not available) (1960-1961) (D)

150 LI 2s. - Dawn Grey 8019 with side-panels, front cowling Flaminia Blue 8032 (1959-1960)

150 LI 2s. - Dawn Grey 8019 with side-panels, front cowling Ruby Red 8047 (1959-1960)

150 LI 2s. - Dawn Grey 8019 with side-panels, front cowling Nile Green 8015 (1959-1960)

150 LI 2s. - Dawn Grey 8019 with side-panels, front cowling England Blue 8031 (1959-1960)

150 LI 2s. - Whitethorn 8082 with side-panels, front cowling Flaminia Blue 8032 (1960-1961)

150 LI 2s. - Whitethorn 8082 with side-panels, front cowling Ruby Red 8047 (1960-1961)

150 LI 2s. - Whitethorn 8082 with side-panels, front cowling Nile Green 8015 (1960-1961)

150 LI 2s. - Whitethorn 8082 with side-panels, front cowling England Blue 8031 (1960-1961)

150 LI 2s. - Whitethorn 8082 with side-panels, front cowling Orange Yellow (colour not available) (1960-1961) (D)

150 LI 2s. - Opal Green (colour not available) (1960-1961) (D)

72 - 175 TV 3s. - New White 8059

175 TV 3s. - Grey 1962 with side-panels, front cowling and front mudguard Coral Red (colour not available) (C) (1963 D)

175 TV 3s. - Grey 1962 with side-panels, front cowling and front mudguard Dark Grey 8071 (C) (1963 D)

175 TV 3s. - New White 8059 with side-panels, front cowling and front mudguard Coral Red 8047 (C) (1963 D)

175 TV 3s. - Grey 1962 with side-panels, front cowling and front mudguard Light Yellow 8064 (C) (1963 D)

175 TV 3s. - New White 8059 with side-panels, front cowling and front mudguard Coral Red (colour not available) (1962

175 TV 3s. - New White 8059 with side-panels, front cowling and front mudguard Ruby Red 8047 (from 1963)

175 TV 3s. - New White 8059 with side-panels, front cowling and front mudguard Dark Grey 8071

175 TV 3s. - New White 8059 with side-panels, front cowling and front mudguard Light Yellow 8064

175 TV 3s. - New White 8059 with side-panels and front cowling New Blue 8059 (D)

175 TV 3s. - New White 8059 with side-panels and front cowling Nile Green 8015 (D)

175 TV 3s. - Metallic Blue 8062 (from 1964)

125 LI3s. - Iseo Blue 8035

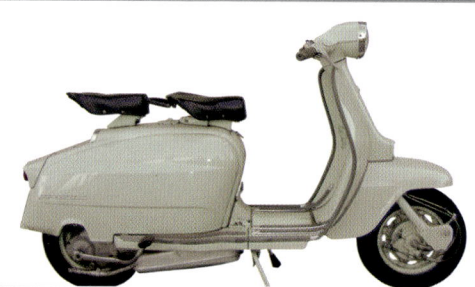
125 LI 3s. - Beige (colour not available)

125 LI 3s. - Extra-light Blue (colour not available) (from 1964)

150 LI3s. - Grey 8068 with side-panels and front cowling New Blue (C)

150 LI 3s. - Grey 8068 with side-panels and front cowling Ruby Red 8047 (C)

150 LI 3s. - Grey 8068 with side-panels and front cowling Nile Green 8015 (C)

150 LI 3s. - New White 8059 with side-panels and front cowling New Blue 8059

150 LI 3s. - New White 8059 with side-panels and front cowling Ruby Red 8047

150 LI 3s. - New White 8059 with side-panels and front cowling Nile Green 8015

150 LI 3s. - Ruby Red 8047 (D)

150 LI 3s. - Sand Beige (colour not available) (D)

150 LISX - Whitethorn 8082 with side-panels and leg-shield Ischia Blue (colour not available) (D)

150 LISX - Red 8073 (D)

150 LISX - Ochre 8080 (D)

150 S - Metallic Grey 8060

150 S - Light Metallic Gold 8063 (from 1965)

125 S - Metallic Light Blue 8061

125 S - Whitethorn 8082 (A) (B)

150 SX - Spring Grey 8070

150 SX - Apple Green 8339

150 SX - Whitethorn 8082 (B)

150 SX - Whitethorn 8082 and side-panels Ischia Blue (colour not available) (D)

150 SX - Special Orange (A) (B)

200 SX - New White 8059

200 SX - Whitethorn 8082 (A) (B)

200 SX - Ochre 8080 (A) (B)

125 DL - Turquoise 8016

125 DL - Whitethorn 8082

150 DL - Red 8073

150 DL - Whitethorn 8082

150 DL - Whitethorn 8082 with side-panels and front cowling Ischia Blue (colour not available) (D)

200 DL - Ochre 8080

200 DL - Whitethorn 8082 (A)

200 DL - Red 8073 (D)

100J - Light Ivory 8054

100 J - Light Blue (colour not available)

125 J 3m - Metallic Grey 8060

125 J 3m - Metallic Light Blue 8062

125 J 3m - Light Olive Green 8079 (D)

125 J 3m - Roman Blue (colour not available) (D)

125 J 4m - Light Blue 04T Pastel Blue A

125 J 4m - New White 8059

125 J SS - New White 8059 with side-panels, front cowling and mudguard New Blue 8038 (D)

125 J SS - New White 8059 with side-panels, front cowling and mudguard Red 8047 (D)

50 J '64 - New White 8059

50 J '64 - Light Olive Green 8079 with side-panels Dark Olive Green 8078

50 J'64 - New White 8059 with side-panels Ruby Red 8047 (1965-1966)

50 J'64 - New White 8059 with side-panels New Blue 8038 (1965-1966)

50 J'64 - Ruby Red 8047 (1966) (A)

50 J'66 - New White 8059

50 J'66 - Aquamarine Blue 8030

50 J'66 - Apple Green 8039

50 J'66 - Special Purple (colour not available) (1967) (A)

50 J'66 - Special Green (colour not available) (1967) (A)

50 J'66 - Special Orange (colour not available) (1967) (A)

50 DL - Whitethorn 8082

50 DL - Apple Green 8039

50 DL - Aquamarine Blue 8030

50 S 8016 - Turquoise 8016

50 S - Red 8073

50 S - Ochre 8080

50 C - Whitethorn 8082

50 CL - Orange 8037

50 CL - Turquoise 8016

50 CL - Apple Green 8039

75 S - Metallic Grey 8060

75 S - Ochre 8080

75 S - Red 8073 (D)

75 S - Light Metallic Gold 8063 (D)

48 - Pompei Red 8045

48 - Earth Grey 8041

48 - Lambro Grey 8034

TECHNICAL DATA

MODEL	A	B	C	LC	E	F	D 125	LD 125 (16)	D 150
Year (1)	1947 - 1948	1948 - 1950	1950 - 1951	1950 - 1951	1953 - 1954	1954 - 1955	1953 - 1955	1953 - 1958	1954 - 1957
Factory	INNOCENTI	INNOCENTI	INNOCENTI	INNOCENTI	INNOCENTI	INNOCENTI	INNOCENTI	INNOCENTI	INNOCENTI
Type (2)	LAMBRETTA 125 A	LAMBRETTA 125 B	LAMBRETTA 125 C	LAMBRETTA 125 LC	LAMBRETTA 125 E	LAMBRETTA 125 F	LAMBRETTA 125 D	LAMBRETTA 125 LD	LAMBRETTA 150 D
Homologation (3)	183 _ 29/10/1951	-	83 _ 16/02/1951	51 _ 01/09/1950	302 _ 09/03/1953	-	221 _ 01/04/1952	222 _ 01/04/1952	403 _ 08/11/1954
Vehicle type	MOTORCYCLE	MOTORCYCLE	MOTORCYCLE	MOTORCYCLE	MOTORCYCLE	MOTORCYCLE	MOTORCYCLE	MOTORCYCLE	MOTORCYCLE
Category	L3	L3	L3	L3	L3	L3	L3	L3	L3
Frame number prefix	\	\	125 C	\	125 E	125 F	125 D	125 LD	150 D
Location	Near upper engine support	Near upper engine support	Under front engine support, left side	Under front engine support, left side	Frame pipe under the saddle, right side	Frame pipe under the saddle, right side	rear descending frame pipe, right side; some on the saddle support, right side	rear descending frame pipe, right side; some on the saddle support, right side	Frame pipe under the tank, right side
Identification plate	\	\	\	\	\	\	\	\	\
Engine number prefix	Type 2	Type B	125 C	125 LC	125 E	125 F	125 D	125 LD	150 D
Engine type	Type 2	Type B	125 C	125 LC	125 e	125 f	125 D	125 LD	150 D
Stroke and fuel	2 - oil/gas mix	2 - oil/gas mix	2 - oil/gas mix	2 - oil/gas mix	2 - oil/gas mix	2 - oil/gas mix	2 - oil/gas mix	2 - oil/gas mix	2 - oil/gas mix
Displacemente	123	123	123	123	123	123	123	123	148
Bore	52	52	52	52	52	52	52	52	57
Stroke	58	58	58	58	58	58	58	58	58
Power CV	4,2	4,3	4,2	4,2	3,68	3,68	5,22	5,22	6,05
Power KW	3,09	3,09	3,09	3,09	2,7	2,7	3,84	3,84	4,45
Rpm	4400	4400	4400	4400	4000	4000	4750	4750	4600
Maximum speed	68	68	68	68	75	75	78	75	80
Transmission	direct	direct	direct	direct	direct	direct	direct	direct	direct
Gearbox	manual	manual	manual	manual	manual	manual	manual	manual	manual
Clutch	mechanical drive	mechanical drive	mechanical drive	mechanical drive	mechanical drive	mechanical drive	mechanical drive	mechanical drive	mechanical drive
Clutch type	multiple discs	multiple discs	multiple discs	multiple discs	multiple discs	multiple discs	multiple discs	multiple discs	multiple discs
Final ratio	4,17	4,8	4,8	4,8	4,93	4,93	4,75	4,75	4,75
Gears number	3	3	3	3	3	3	3	3	3
Brakes	mechanical	mechanical	mechanical	mechanical	mechanical	mechanical	mechanical	mechanical	mechanical
Parking brake	\	\	\	\	\	\	\	\	\
Total weight (4)	222	222	220	235	212	212	229	243	230
Tare (5)	147	147	145	160	137	137	154	168	155
Lenght	1,62	1,66	1,73	1,74	1,76	1,76	1,77	1,77	1,77
Width	0,74	0,77	0,76	0,76	0,71	0,71	0,74	0,74	0,74
Axles	2	2	2	2	2	2	2	2	2
Wheelbase	1,22	1,26	1,24	1,24	1,28	1,28	1,28	1,28	1,28
Front overhang (6)	0,18	0,19	0,2	0,2	0,2	0,2	0,2	0,2	0,2
Rear overhang (6)	0,22	0,21	0,27	0,28	0,28	0,28	0,29	0,29	0,29
Track (7)	\	\	\	\	\	\	\	\	\
Front tyre	3,5 x 7	3,5 x 8	4,0 x 8	4,0 x 8	4,0 x 8	4,0 x 8	4,0 x 8	4,0 x 8	4,0 x 8
Rear tyre	3,5 x 7	3,5 x 8	4,0 x 8	4,0 x 8	4,0 x 8	4,0 x 8	4,0 x 8	4,0 x 8	4,0 x 8
Third wheel tyre (7)	\	\	\	\	\	\	\	\	\
Front suspension	rubber coupling	coil springs	coil springs	coil springs	leaf springs	leaf springs	coil springs	coil springs	coil springs
Rear suspension	absent	coil springs	coil springs	coil springs	torsion bar	torsion bar	torsion bar	torsion bar	torsion bar
Shock absorbers	\	\	\	\	\	\	\	\	telescopic
Seats (8)	2	2	2	2	2	2	2	2	2
Lighting devices	(20)	(20)	(20)	(20)	(20)	(20)	(20)	(20)	(20)
Mirrors	Left	Left	Left	Left	Left	Left	Left	Left	Left
Exhaust silencer (9)	Compliant	Compliant	Compliant	Compliant	App. IGM 112/S	App. IGM 112/S	App. IGM 503/S (18)	App. IGM 496/S	App. IGM 502/S

Edited by Daniele Rey, ASI-Lambretta Club Italia Representative

150 (7)	LI 125 FIRST SERIES	LI 150 FIRST SERIES	TV 175 FIRST SERIES	LI 125 SECOND SERIES	LI 150 SECOND SERIES	TV 175 SECOND SERIES	LI 125 THIRD SERIES (10)	LI 150 T THIRD SERIES	TV 175 THIRD SERIES	SPECIAL 125
1954 - 1958	1958 - 1959	1958 - 1959	1957 - 1958	1959 - 1961	1959 - 1961	1959 - 1961	1951 - 1967	1951 - 1967	1962 - 1965	1965 - 1969
INNOCENTI	INNOCENTI	INNOCENTI	INNOCENTI	INNOCENTI	INNOCENTI	INNOCENTI	INNOCENTI	INNOCENTI	INNOCENTI	INNOCENTI
LAMBRETTA 150 LD	LAMBRETTA 125 LI	LAMBRETTA 150 LI	LAMBRETTA 175 TV	LAMBRETTA 125 LI	LAMBRETTA 150 LI	LAMBRETTA 175 TV/2° SERIES	LAMBRETTA 125 LI	LAMBRETTA 150 LI	LAMBRETTA 175 TV	LAMBRETTA 125 LI SPECIAL
48 _ 24/04/1955	1009/58/0	917/58/0	-	IGM 0901 OM (17)	IGM 0903 OM (17)	1130/58/0 later IGM 0904 OM	IGM 0901 OM	IGM 0903 OM	IGM 2515 OM	IGM 4190 OM
MOTORCYCLE	MOTORCYCLE	MOTORCYCLE	MOTORCYCLE	MOTORCYCLE	MOTORCYCLE	MOTORCYCLE	MOTORCYCLE	MOTORCYCLE	MOTORCYCLE	MOTORCYCLE
3	L3	L3	L3	L3	L3	L3	L3	L3	L3	L3
150 LD	125 LI	150 LI	175 TV1	125 LI	150 LI	175 TV/2	125 LI 3 - 125 LI 4 (10)	150 LI 3	175 TV/3	125 LIS
Frame pipe under the tank, right side	Frame pipe under the tank, right side	Frame pipe under the tank, right side	Frame pipe under the tank, right side	Frame pipe under the tank, right side	Frame pipe under the tank, right side	Frame pipe under the tank, right side	Frame pipe under the tank, right side	Frame pipe under the tank, right side	Frame pipe under the tank, right side	Frame pipe under the tank, right side
\	\	\	\	\	\	\	\	\	\	\
150 LD	125 LI	150 LI	175 TV1	125 LI	150 LI	175 TV/2	125 LI	150 LI	175 TV/2	125 LIS
150 LD	125 LI	150 LI	175 TV1	125 LI	150 LI	175 TV/2	125 LI	150 LI	175 TV/2	125 LIS
- oil/gas mix	2 - oil/gas mix	2 - oil/gas mix	2 - oil/gas mix	2 - oil/gas mix	2 - oil/gas mix	2 - oil/gas mix	2 - oil/gas mix	2 - oil/gas mix	2 - oil/gas mix	2 - oil/gas mix
148	123,1	148	170	123,1	148	175,09	123	148	175	123
57	52	57	60	52	57	62	52	57	62	52
58	58	58	60	58	58	58	58	58	58	58
6,05	5,29	6,67	8,6	5,29	6,67	8,75	5,29	6,67	8,75	7,12
4,5	3,89	4,9	6,32	3,89	4,9	6,44	3,89	4,9	6,44	5,24
4600	5000	5200	6000	5000	5200	5300	5000	5200	5300	5500
74	79	83	103	79	83	104	79	83	104	75
direct	direct	direct	direct	direct	direct	direct	direct	direct	direct	direct
manual	manual	manual	manual	manual	manual	manual	manual	manual	manual	manual
mechanical drive	mechanical drive	mechanical drive	mechanical drive	mechanical drive	mechanical drive	mechanical drive	mechanical drive	mechanical drive	mechanical drive	mechanical drive
multiple discs	multiple discs	multiple discs	multiple discs	multiple discs	multiple discs	multiple discs	multiple discs	multiple discs	multiple discs	multiple discs
75	5,65	5,21	4,81	5,67	5,21	4,81	5, 67 - 5,64 (10)	5,21	4,81	6,13
4	4	4	4	4	4	4	4	4	4	4
mechanical	mechanical	mechanical	mechanical	mechanical	mechanical	mechanical	mechanical	mechanical	mechanical	mechanical
\	\	\	\	\	\	\	\	\	\	\
243	268	270	270	265	268	273	265	268	273	265
58	193	195	195	193	195	198	193	195	198	193
1,77	1,83	1,83	1,83	1,83	1,83	1,83	1,8	1,8	1,8	1,8
0,74	0,72	0,72	0,72	0,71	0,72	0,71	0,7	0,7	0,7	0,7
2	2	2	2	2	2	2	2	2	2	2
1,28	1,3	1,29	1,29	1,3	1,29	1,29	1,29	1,29	1,29	1,29
2	0,21	0,21	0,21	0,21	0,21	0,21	0,21	0,21	0,21	0,21
29	0,33	0,33	0,33	0,33	0,33	0,33	0,3	0,3	0,3	0,3
\	\	\	\	\	\	\	\	\	\	\
10 x 8	3,5 X 10	3,5 X 10	3,5 X 10	3,5 X 10	3,5 X 10	3,5 X 10	3,5 X 10	3,5 X 10	3,5 X 10	3,5 X 10
10 x 8	3,5 X 10	3,5 X 10	3,5 X 10	3,5 X 10	3,5 X 10	3,5 X 10	3,5 X 10	3,5 X 10	3,5 X 10	3,5 X 10
\	\	\	\	\	\	\	\	\	\	\
coil springs	coil springs	coil springs	coil springs	coil springs	coil springs	coil springs	coil springs	coil springs	coil springs	coil springs
torsion bar	coil springs	coil springs	coil springs	coil springs	coil springs	coil springs	coil springs	coil springs	coil springs	coil springs
telescopic	telescopic	telescopic	telescopic	telescopic	telescopic	telescopic	telescopic	telescopic	telescopic	telescopic
2	2	2	2	2	2	2	2	2	2	2
(20)	(20)	(20)	(20)	(20)	(20)	(20)	(20)	(20)	(20)	(20)
Left	Left	Left	Left and right	Left	Left	Left and right	Left	Left	Left and right	Left
App. IGM 503/S	App. IGM 880/58/S or INNOCENTI SC20-IGM 0277 S	App. IGM 880/58/S or INNOCENTI SC20-IGM 0277 S		INNOCENTI SC20-IGM 0277 S	INNOCENTI SC20-IGM 0277 S	App. IGM 1131/58/S or INNOCENTI SC20-IGM 0277 S	INNOCENTI SC21-IGM 2105 S	INNOCENTI-SC21-IGM 2105 S	INNOCENTI-SC21-IGM 2105 S	INNOCENTI-SC21-IGM 2105 S SC21-IGM 2105 S

TECHNICAL DATA

MODEL	SPECIAL 150	SPECIAL 150 (SPAIN)	SX 150	SX 200	200 JET (SPAIN)	DL 125	DL 150	DL 150 (INDIA)	DL 200
Year (1)	1963 - 1966	1972 - 1985	1966 - 1969	1966 - 1969	1972 - 1985	1969 - 1971	1969 - 1971	1973 - 1998	1969 - 1971
Factory	INNOCENTI	SERVETA INDUSTRIAL	INNOCENTI	INNOCENTI	SERVETA INDUSTRIAL	INNOCENTI	INNOCENTI	SIL (SCOOTERS INDIA LIMITED)	INNOCENTI
	LAMBRETTA 150	LAMBRETTA 150	LAMBRETTA	LAMBRETTA	LAMBRETTA	LAMBRETTA	LAMBRETTA 150 DL		LAMBRETTA 200 DL
Type (2)	LI SPECIAL	LI SPECIAL	SPECIAL X 150	SPECIAL X 200	200 SX JET	125 DL		150 DL	
Homologation (3)	IGM 3316 OM	OM 16446 (14)	IGM 4770 OM	IGM 4355 OM	OM 16445 (14)	DGM 6439 OM	DGM 6437 OM	OM 16918 (14)	DGM 6441 OM
Vehicle type	MOTORCYCLE	MOTORCYCLE	MOTORCYCLE	MOTORCYCLE	MOTORCYCLE	MOTORCYCLE	MOTORCYCLE	MOTORCYCLE	MOTORCYCLE
Category	L3	L3	L3	L3	L3	L3	L3	L3	L3
Frame number prefix	150 LIS	\	SX 150	SX 200	SX 200	22/1	22/0	05	22/2
Location	Frame pipe under the fuel-tank, right side	Frame pipe under the fuel-tank, right side	Frame pipe under the fuel-tank, right side	Frame pipe under the fuel-tank, right side	Frame pipe under the fuel-tank, right side	Frame pipe under the fuel-tank, right side	Frame pipe under the fuel-tank, right side	Frame pipe under the fuel-tank, right side	Frame pipe under the fuel-tank, right side
Identification plate	\	\	\	\	\	\	\	(15)	\
Engine number prefix	150 LI (19)	150 LI	SX 150	SX 200	SX 200	125 LIS	SX 150	005	SX 200
Engine type	150 LI (19)	150 LI	SX 150	SX 200	SX 200	125 LIS	SX 150	005	SX 200
Stroke and fuel	2 - oil/gas mix	2 - oil/gas mix	2 - oil/gas mix	2 - oil/gas mix	2 - oil/gas mix	2 - oil/gas mix	2 - oil/gas mix	2 - oil/gas mix	2 - oil/gas mix
Displacement	148	148	148	198	198	123	148	148	198
Bore	57	57	57	66	66	52	57	57	66
Stroke	58	58	58	58	58	58	58	58	58
Power CV	8,25	6	9,38	11	9,52	7,4	9,4	9	11,9
Power KW	6,07	4,41	6,9	8,09	7	5,44	6,91	6,62	8,75
Rpm	5590	5000	5600	5500	5500	6200	6300	5900	6200
Maximum speed	92	90	97	107	105	91,5	100,5	102	110,8
Transmission	direct	direct	direct	direct	direct	direct	direct	direct	direct
Gearbox	manual	manual	manual	manual	manual	manual	manual	manual	manual
Clutch	mechanical drive	mechanical drive	mechanical drive	comando mecc.	mechanical drive	mechanical drive	mechanical drive	mechanical drive	mechanical drive
Clutch type	multiple discs	multiple discs	multiple discs	multiple discs	multiple discs	multiple discs	multiple discs	multiple discs	multiple discs
Final ratio	5,65	5,21	5,65	4,81	4,81	6,13	5,65	5,65	5,22
Gears number	4	4	4	4	4	4	4	4	4
Brakes	mechanical	mechanical	mechanical	mechanical	mechanical	mechanical	mechanical	mechanical	mechanical
Parking brake	\	\	\	\	\	\	\	\	\
Total weight (4)	270	270	270	273	273	268	268	265	273
Tare (5)	195	195	195	198	198	193	193	195	198
Lenght	1,8	1,8	1,8	1,8	1,8	1,8	1,8	1,8	1,8
Width	0,7	0,7	0,7	0,7	0,7	0,68	0,68	0,7	0,68
Axles	2	2	2	2	2	2	2	2	2
Wheelbase	1,29	1,29	1,29	1,29	1,29	1,29	1,29	1,29	1,29
Front overhang (6)	0,21	0,21	0,21	0,21	0,21	0,21	0,21	0,21	0,21
Rear overhang (6)	0,3	0,3	0,3	0,3	0,3	0,3	0,3	0,3	0,3
Track (7)	\	\	\	\	\	\	\	\	\
Front tyre	3,5 X 10	3,5 X 10	3,5 X 10	3,5 X 10	3,5 X 10	3,5 X 10	3,5 X 10	3,5 X 10	3,5 X 10
Rear tyre	3,5 X 10	3,5 X 10	3,5 X 10	3,5 X 10	3,5 X 10	3,5 X 10	3,5 X 10	3,5 X 10	3,5 X 10
Third wheel tyre (7)	\	\	\	\	\	\	\	\	\
Front suspension	coil springs	coil springs	coil springs	coil springs	coil springs	coil springs	coil springs	coil springs	coil springs
Rear suspension	coil springs	coil springs	coil springs	coil springs	coil springs	coil springs	coil springs	coil springs	coil springs
Shock absorbers	telescopic	telescopic	telescopic	telescopic	telescopic	telescopic	telescopic	telescopic	telescopic
Seats (8)	2	2	2	2	2	2	2	2	2
Lighting devices	(20)	(22)	(20)	(20)	(22)	(20)	(20)	(22)	(20)
Mirrors	Left	Left	Left	Left and right	Left and right	Left	Left and right	Left and right	Left and right
Exhaust silencer (9)	INNOCENTI-SC21-IGM 2105 S	32049 S	INNOCENTI-SC21-IGM 2105 S	INNOCENTI-SC21-IGM 2105 S	32049 S	INNOCENTI-SC21-IGM 2105 S	INNOCENTI-SC21-IGM 2105 S	32049 S	INNOCENTI-SC21-IGM 2105 S

	JUNIOR 50	JUNIOR 50	JUNIOR 50 DL	JUNIOR 100	JUNIOR 125	JUNIOR 125	LUI 50	LUI 75	CICLO MOTORE 48	LAMBRETTINO 39	LAMBRETTINO SX
		FIRST SERIES 50	SECOND SERIES	Special	FIRST SERIES	SECOND SERIES					
	1964 - 1966	1966 - 1968	1968 - 1971	1964 - 1965	1964 - 1966	1966 - 1968	1968 - 1969	1968 - 1969	1955 - 1961	1966 - 1968	1966 - 1968
	INNOCENTI	INNOCENTI	INNOCENTI	INNOCENTI	INNOCENTI	INNOCENTI	INNOCENTI	INNOCENTI	INNOCENTI	INNOCENTI	INNOCENTI
	LAMBRETTA J50	LAMBRETTA J50	LAMBRETTA J50 DL/S		LAMBRETTA J 125	LAMBRETTA J 125	LAMBRETTA 50 C	LAMBRETTA 75 S LUI	LAMBRETTA 48 8	LAMBRETTINO 21/50	LAMBRETTINO SX
	IGM 3687 OM	IGM 3687 OM	DGM 5520 OM	IGM 3484 oM	IGM 3689 OM	IGM 3689 OM	DGM 5629 OM	DGM 6126 OM	-	IGM 4837 OM	IGM 5353 OM
	MOPED	MOPED	MOPED	MOTOVEICOLO	MOTORCYCLE	MOTORCYCLE	MOPED	MOTOVEICOLO	MOPED	MOPED	MOPED
	L1	L1	L1	L3	L3	L3	L1	L3	L1	L1	L1
	J 50	J 50	50 D.L.	100 LB	J 125	J125	20/9	20/8	48 A (12)	21/50	21/9
	Edge of the body on the engine, right side	Edge of the body on the engine, right side	Edge of the body on the engine, right side	Edge of the body on the engine, right side	Edge of the body on the engine, right side	Edge of the body on the engine, right side	Near left engine support	Near left engine support	Between engine supports, left side	Rear wheel right support arm	Rear wheel right support arm
	\	\	\	\	\	\	\	\	\	\	\
	J 50 (13)	J 50 (13)	J 50 (13)	J 100	J 125	J 125	J 50 (13)	75 S	48 A (12)	-	-
	J 50 (13)	J 50 (13)	J 50 (13)	J 100	J 125	J125	J 50 (13)	75 S	48 A	-	-
	2 - oil/gas mix	2 - oil/gas mix	2 - oil/gas mix	2 - oil/gas mix	2 - oil/gas mix	2 - oil/gas mix	2 - oil/gas mix	2 - oil/gas mix	2 - oil/gas mix	2 - oil/gas mix	2 - oil/gas mix
	49,8	49,8	49,8	98	122,48	122,48	49,8	74,4	47,75	39	48,5
	38	38	38	51	57	57	38	46,4	40	40	41,4
	44	44	44	48	48	48	44	44	38	31	36
	1,47	1,47	1,47	4,7	5,8	5,8	1,48	5	1,7	1,26	1,27
	1,08	1,08	1,08	3,45	4,26	4,26	1,08	3,68	1,25	0,92	0,93
	4500	4500	4500	5300	5300	5300	4600	6300	5000	4500	4400
	40	40	40	76	86,7	87	37,1	82,5	45	38,9	37,9
	direct	direct	direct	direct	direct	direct	direct	direct	chain	chain	chain
	manual	manual	manual	manual	manual	manual	manual	manual	manual	direct	automatic variator
	mechanical drive	mechanical drive	mechanical drive	mechanical drive	mechanical drive	mechanical drive	mechanical drive	mechanical drive	mechanical drive	automatic	automatic
	multiple discs	multiple discs	multiple discs	multiple discs	multiple discs	multiple discs	multiple discs	multiple discs	multiple discs	automatic	automatic
	8,65	8,65	9,82	5,97	5,66	5,75	9,83	6,9	?	0,05	0,06
	3	3	3	3	3	4	3	4	2	1	\
	mechanical	mechanical	mechanical	mechanical	mechanical	mechanical	mechanical	mechanical	mechanical	mechanical	mechanical
	\	\	\	\	\	\	\	\	\	\	\
	153	153	153	240	240	240	143,5	227	119	115,7	115,7
	153	153	153	165	165	165	143,5	152	119	115,7	115,7
	1,66	1,66	1,66	1,69	1,69	1,69	1,7	1,69	1,9	1,65	1,65
	0,63	0,63	0,63	0,63	0,63	0,63	0,63	0,66	69	0,65	0,65
	2	2	2	2	2	2	2	2	2	2	2
	1,19	1,19	1,19	1,19	1,19	1,19	1,2	1,2	1,19	1,05	1,05
	0,2	0,2	0,2	0,2	0,2	0,2	0,2	0,2	0,34	0,29	0,29
	0,27	0,27	0,27	0,3	0,3	0,3	0,3	0,29	0,37	0,31	0,31
	\	\	\	\	\	\	\	\	\	\	\
	2,75 X 9	2,75 X 9 (11)	3,00 X 10	3,00 X 10	3,00 X 10	3,00 X 10	3,00 X 10	3,00 X 10	2 X 22	2 X 18	2 X 18
	2,75 X 9	2,75 X 9 (11)	3,00 X 10	3,00 X 10	3,00 X 10	3,00 X 10	3,00 X 10	3,00 X 10	2 X 22	2 X 18	2 X 18
	\	\	\	\	\	\	\	\	\	\	\
	coil springs	coil springs	coil springs	coil springs	coil springs	coil springs	coil springs	coil springs	coil springs	coil springs	coil springs
	coil springs	coil springs	coil springs	coil springs	coil springs	coil springs	coil springs	coil springs	coil springs	rigid	rigid
	telescopic	telescopic	telescopic	telescopic	telescopic	telescopic	telescopic	telescopic	\	\	\
	1	1	1	1	2	2	2	2	1	1	1
	(21)	(21)	(21)	(20)	(20)	(20)	(21)	(20)	(21)	(21)	(21)
	Left	Left	Left	Left	Left	Left	Left	Left	Left	Left	Left
	INNOCENTI-C23-IGM 3688 S	INNOCENTI-SC23-IGM 3688 S	INNOCENTI-SC23-IGM 3688 S	?	INNOCENTI-ISC22-IGM 3485 S	INNOCENTI-SC22-IGM 3485 S	INNOCENTI-DGM 5630 S	INNOCENTI-DGM 6127 S	App. IGM 778/S	INNOCENTI-GM 4838 S	INNOCENTI-GM 5352 S

* notes: see last page

NOTES

(1) Found on the vehicle documents; should these be missing or should there be any discrepancy consult your club's technical commissioner.
(2) Official names. Always indicate what is recorded on the documents where sufficiently correct.
(3) The homologation codes through to 1960 do not begin with "IGM", "DGM" or "OM" and are not recorded on either the documents or the vehicle.
(4) The overall weight takes into account the passenger. If vehicles constructed through to 1960 are reregistered for use by the driver only, the overall weight is equal to the tare weight.
(5) Weight of the vehicle plus the driver.
(6) Recorded, non-official data.
(7) Concerns delivery trucks and scooter combinations.
(8) Vehicles constructed prior to 1960 may be reregistered for use by the driver only. Indicating "2" on the model for CRS a saddle, footboards and handles must be fitted for the passenger.
(9) If you do not have a silencer with the correct homologation code, consult your club technical commissioner.
(10) The last of the third series LI 125s to be produced, distinguished by the frame prefix 125LI4 and commonly known as the "fourth series", use a different gearbox.
(11) The last of the second series J50s were factory-fitted with 3.00x10 tyres. No official documentation to this effect is currently available.
(12) The first series versions (single gearbox cable) carry the 48A prefix. The second series versions (dual gearbox cable) have no prefix.
(13) The engines fitted to the Junior 50 and the Lui 50 are different but both carry the J50 code.
(14) Homologation recorded on the registration document but not the frame.
(15) In some cases found under the toolbox lid.
(16) No official documentation is currently available regarding homologation variations to this model during its evolution.
(17) The second series LI is a transitional model. The first examples through to 1960 have an unknown homologation and do not carry homologation data on either the frame or the registration document; the last examples are IGM homologated.
(18) The precise homologation code of the LD 125 exhaust is not known, but it is officially permitted to fit the LD 150 exhaust.
(19) The engine should be marked 150LIS, as per the homologation sheet and as generally indicated on the documents. In reality, all the engines for this model are exclusively marked 150 LI.
(20) Indicate: Main beam 1 white _ Main beam 1 white – Position Front 1 white _ Position Rear 1 red – Stop light 1 red – Rear reflector 1 red – Number plate light 1 white _ Note homologation codes on lamps (where present)
(21) Indicate: Dipped 1 white _ Position Front 1 white _ Position Rear 1 red _ Rear reflector 1 red _ Note homologation codes on lamps (where present)
(22) As for note (20), in addition indicate (where present): Indicators Front 2 orange _ Indicators Rear 2 orange

Printed by Grafiche Flaminia - Foligno (PG)
January 2012